EX LIBRIS

Two Complete Works

LETTERS TO A
YOUNG POET

THE POSSIBILITY
OF BEING

Rainer Maria Rilke

FOREWORD BY KENT NERBURN

**BARNES
&NOBLE
BOOKS**
NEW YORK

Published by MJF Books
Fine Communications
322 Eighth Avenue
New York, NY 10001

Letters to a Young Poet/ Possibility of Being
Library of Congress Control No. 2002100594
ISBN 1-56731-520-8

Grateful acknowledgement is made to Professor Theodore Ziolkowski of Princeton
University, who chose the current selection of poems from the various New Directions
volumes of Rilke's work translated by J.B. Leishman. Portions of this selection appear by
arrangement with W.W. Norton & Company, Inc.

LETTERS TO A
Young Poet

RAINER MARIA RILKE

Translated by
Joan M. Burnham

Foreword by
Kent Nerburn

❦

For one human being to love another is
perhaps the most difficult task of all,
the epitome, the ultimate test.
It is that striving for which all other striving
is merely preparation.

Rainer Maria Rilke

Contents

◈

FOREWORD

All of us who labor in the arts know that it can be a lonely existence. We often find ourselves living a life of solitary dreams, disconnected from others, and driven by a vision that no one else seems to value or share. On some days, this can become overwhelming. We then thirst for a single voice of understanding that will reach into our solitary lives and reassure us that the path we have chosen is worthy, and that the rewards it offers are worth the loneliness it entails.

For almost a hundred years, the voice that has reached out to the aspiring artist with the most clarity and consolation is that of Rainer Maria Rilke. And the place where his voice speaks most clearly is in the transcendently insightful small volume *Letters to a Young Poet*.

It is a deceptively simple book. It consists of ten short letters, written over a five-year period to an aspiring young poet named Franz Xaver Kappus. The letters range freely over a variety of subjects, from the dangers of an ironic worldview to the value of faith and the close link between physical and creative ecstasy. But, always, they come back to the fundamental theme of the aloneness of the creative spirit, and the demands it makes upon the lives of those who labor in its service.

How is it that such a slim book, written so many years ago in a time so very different from our own, still speaks to us with such authority today? It is easy to point to Rilke's personal genius. And, to be sure, that plays a part. But if we look past this obvious source, we see that these letters are also the result of a unique conjunction of circumstances that created an almost magical alchemy of thought and feeling. And it is in this magical alchemy that their enduring significance lies.

The three circumstances that came together to create this alchemy were Rilke's background, his age when he wrote the letters, and the great, looming shadow of the sculptor Auguste Rodin. Rilke came from a background that made him deeply sympathetic to the struggles of anyone striving to be an artist. His father had been a career military man and had sent his son off to a military boarding school with the intention of training him to be an officer. Rilke, weak of constitution and romantic in temperament, was ill suited to the physical rigors and severe discipline at the school, and was subjected to numerous cruelties by his classmates and teachers. Still, he remained there for five formative years of his early adolescence before, humiliated and physically and spiritually exhausted, he was allowed to return to his native Prague to continue his studies at home. During these five trying years he found his greatest solace and self-expression in the act of writing poetry. It was his only means of shaping what he called the "damnation" of those years into something of meaning and beauty.

So, when young Franz Kappus wrote him from that same military academy a dozen years later, asking for advice on how to go about living the life of an artist, it touched a chord so deep in Rilke that he could not do otherwise than to write from the most honest place in his heart about the travails and loneliness of the artist's life in a difficult and unsympathetic world.

Rilke's age at the time he wrote the letters also had a deep effect on their enduring power. Because of their depth of sentiment and sense of wise detachment, readers often assume they are the work of an older man looking back on the struggles of his youth. But, in fact, these letters were written between Rilke's twenty-eighth and thirty-third years — years in which he was struggling to find himself artistically, embarking on a marriage, traveling, and meeting life with that freshness that only offers itself to us in the years of early adulthood. He was a grown man in full command of his intellectual powers, but he was also a young man alive with the passions of youthful discovery. And this gives his insights about life, love, and art an immediacy and authenticity that can only come from one in whom the very same emotions are alive and present.

But it is the great, overarching shadow of the French sculptor Auguste Rodin that in the last analysis may prove to be the leavening agent that lifts Rilke's insights from the profound observations of a sensitive and talented young man to the status of timeless utterances about the mysteries of life and the creative process.

In 1902, the year before the first of these letters to Franz Kappus, Rilke had come to Paris with the intention of writing a monograph on Rodin. His wife, Clara, a sculptor, was to study with the master, and it was an opportunity for Rilke to observe first hand the workings of genius, which he so desperately wanted to find in himself.

Rodin was everything Rilke was not — confident, robust, sensual, an older man who was secure in his artistic identity and accomplished in his artistic voice. He was an elemental presence, with a chiseled brow, a laborer's broad physique, and piercing eyes that seemed to see through the artifice and brittle surface of anyone on whom he chose to focus his attention. He was also a man of few words who worked with unceasing diligence, and thought, felt, and spoke not through his words but through the creations of his hands. As Rilke himself said, Rodin lived inside his art; he did not have to constantly seek it and court it from amongst the intrusive distractions of daily affairs.

Contrasted to this was Rilke, the fragile, often sickly young man of delicate sensibilities and uncertain artistic direction, who suffered long periods of artistic aridity and terrifying self-doubt. Slim, slight, easily led astray from his artistic tasks, he lived in constant fear of days when all inspiration failed him and he was left with nothing but "dead words...corpse heavy."

How could he not stand in the presence of Rodin without seeing before him the embodiment of all he desired to be as an artist, as well as a mirror of all his own artistic deficiencies and insecurities? And, in fact, this is exactly what happened. In the person of Rodin, Rilke found the model for the artistic authority he wished to possess. And in the letters to young Franz Kappus, he appropriates this air of authority, which he wears like a mantle over the doubts and insecurities that the letters themselves address. He becomes, at once, the wise and resolved artist he dreams of being, while carrying within himself the visceral knowledge of all the struggles the young artist experiences. He manages to claim, in the way only the greatest artists can, the moral authority of that which he observes, while keeping the emotional authenticity of his own feelings.

When young Kappus reaches out to him from within the very halls of the military academy that had only ten years before almost destroyed his own creative spirit, Rilke finds the perfect opportunity to speak with absolute conviction and the deepest passion about the demons and dreams that confront a young artist struggling in an indifferent and uncaring world. He, in effect, writes from the best part of his own artistic vision to the most fragile part of his own artistic self. We, as readers, can only look on in awe as this brilliant young spirit lays bare the artistic life with a perfect understanding of its deepest desolations and its most exalted ecstasies.

Later in his life, Rilke was to write a beautiful verse on the Archaic Torso of Apollo. Standing before the headless Greek sculpture, so radiant with life despite its fragmentary form, he concludes, "For here, there is no place that does not see you. You must change your life." When any of us, struggling with the dreams and demons of the artistic life, reads these ten brilliant letters on the life of the creative artist, the same shudder of recognition passes through us that passed through Rilke as he stood before the torso of Apollo. We know that from where Rilke writes, there is no place that does not see us. We must change our lives.

Kent Nerburn
Bemidji, Minnesota
January 2000

LETTERS TO A
Young Poet

INTRODUCTION

It was in the late fall of 1902. I was sitting under ancient chestnut trees, in the park of the Military Academy in the new section of Vienna, reading a book. I was so engrossed in the words that I hardly noticed when the learned and beloved chaplain of the academy, the only non-officer on the staff, Professor Horaček, seated himself beside me. He took the volume from my hands, gazed at the cover, and shook his head. "Poems of Rainer Maria Rilke?" he asked thoughtfully. He skimmed the pages, stopping now and then to scan a few verses and gaze pensively into the distance. Finally, with a nod, he said, "Well, René Rilke, my student, has turned into a poet after all."

It was then I learned about the thin, pale boy who had been sent by his parents, more than fifteen years ago, to the Military Academy to become a commissioned officer. At that time Horaček had been chaplain there. He still remembered the former student clearly. He described him as a quiet, serious, highly gifted young man, who liked to keep to himself and who patiently endured the stress of dormitory life. After the fourth year he moved ahead with the others to the military academy in Mahrich-Weisskirchen. There, however, he apparently lacked the necessary endurance for the regimen, so his parents took him out of the school and allowed him to continue his studies at home in Prague. How the events of his life unfolded after that, Professor Horaček could not say.

After our talk, I decided to send Rainer Maria Rilke my poetic attempts and to ask him for his judgment. I was hardly twenty, not quite at the threshold of a career against which I felt an inner revolt. I hoped to receive solace and understanding, if from anyone, from the author of the book *In Celebration of Myself*. Without actually intending it, I found myself writing letters to accompany my verses. In them I revealed my innermost self unreservedly as never before and never since to another person.

Many weeks passed before an answer to the first

letter came. The blue seal revealed the postmark from Paris. It weighed heavy in my hand and revealed on the envelope the same clear, beautiful, and confident handwriting as that in the contents of the letter, from the first line to the last. Thus began my regular correspondence with Rainer Maria Rilke, which lasted until 1908. Gradually it became less frequent and finally stopped because life forced me off into paths from which the poet's gentle, warm, and touching concern would have liked to protect me.

But that is unimportant. Important alone are the ten letters — important for the understanding of the world in which Rainer Maria Rilke lived and worked, important also for the many who are growing and evolving now and shall in the future. When a truly great and unique spirit speaks, the lesser ones must be silent.

Franz Xaver Kappus
Berlin, June 1929

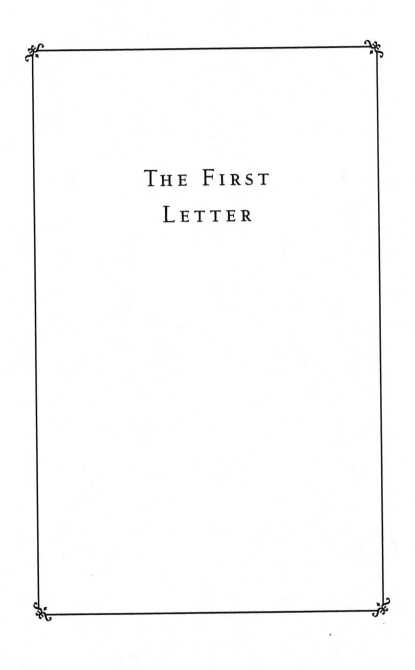

THE FIRST
LETTER

꧁

"I know of no other advice than this:
Go within and scale the depths
of your being from which your very life
springs forth."

Paris
17 February 1903

My dear sir,

Your letter reached me just a few days ago. I want to thank you for the deep and loving trust it revealed. I can do no more. I cannot comment on the style of your verses; critical intent is too far removed from my nature. There is nothing that manages to influence a work of art less than critical words. They always result in more or less unfortunate misunderstandings. Things are not as easily understood nor as expressible as people usually would like us to believe. Most happenings are beyond expression; they exist where a word has never intruded. Even more inexpressible are works of art; mysterious entities they are, whose lives, compared to our fleeting ones, endure.

Having said these things at the outset, I now dare tell you only this: that your verses do not as yet have an individual style. Yet they possess a quiet and hidden inclination to reveal something personal. I felt that very thing most notably in the last poem, "My Soul." There, something of your inner self wants to rise to expression. And in the beautiful poem "To Leopardi" something akin to greatness and bordering on uniqueness is sprouting out toward fulfillment. However, the poems cannot yet stand on their own merit, are not yet independent, not even the last one to Leopardi, not yet. In your kind letter accompanying them, you do not fail to admit to and to analyze some shortcomings, which I could sense while reading your verses, but could not directly put into words.

You ask whether your poems are good. You send them to publishers; you compare them with other poems; you are disturbed when certain publishers reject your attempts. Well now, since you have given me permission to advise you, I suggest that you give all that up. You are looking outward and, above all else, that you must not do now. No one can advise and help you, no one.

There is only one way: Go within. Search for the cause, find the impetus that bids you write. Put it to this test: Does it stretch out its roots in the deepest place of your heart? Can you avow that you would die if you were forbidden to write? Above all, in the most silent hour of your night, ask yourself this: *Must* I write? Dig deep into yourself for a true answer. And if it should ring its assent, if you can confidently meet this serious question with a simple, "I must," then build your life upon it. It has become your necessity. Your life, in even the most mundane and least significant hour, must become a sign, a testimony to this urge.

Then draw near to nature. Pretend you are the very first man and then write what you see and experience, what you love and lose. Do not write love poems, at least at first; they present the greatest challenge. It requires great, fully ripened power to produce something personal, something unique, when there are so many good and sometimes even brilliant renditions in great numbers. Beware of general themes. Cling to those that your everyday life offers you. Write about your sorrows, your wishes, your passing thoughts, your belief in anything beautiful. Describe all that with fervent, quiet, and humble sincerity. In order to express yourself, use things in your surroundings, the scenes of your dreams, and the subjects of your memory.

If your everyday life appears to be unworthy subject matter, do not complain to life. Complain to yourself. Lament that you are not poet enough to call up its wealth. For the creative artist there is no poverty — nothing is insignificant or unimportant. Even if you were in a prison whose walls would shut out from your senses the sounds of the outer world, would you not then still have your childhood, this precious wealth, this treasure house of memories? Direct your attention to that. Attempt to resurrect these sunken sensations of a distant past. You will gain assuredness. Your aloneness will expand and will become your home, greeting you like the quiet dawn. Outer tumult will pass it by from afar.

If, as a result of this turning inward, of this sinking into your own world, *poetry* should emerge, you will not think to ask someone whether it is good poetry. And you will not try to interest publishers of magazines in these works. For you will hear in them your own voice; you will see in them a piece of your life, a natural possession of yours. A piece of art is good if it is born of necessity. This, its source, is its criterion; there is no other.

Therefore, my dear friend, I know of no other advice than this: Go within and scale the depths of your being from which your very life springs forth. At its source you will find the answer to the question, whether you *must* write. Accept it, however it sounds to you, without analyzing. Perhaps it will become apparent to you that you are indeed called to be a writer. Then accept that fate; bear its burden, and its grandeur, without asking for the reward, which might possibly come from without. For the creative artist must be a world of his own and must find everything within himself and in nature, to which he has betrothed himself.

It is possible that, even after your descent into your inner self and into your secret place of solitude, you might find that you must give up becoming a poet. As I have said, to feel that one could live without writing is enough indication that, in fact, one should not. Even then this process of turning inward, upon which I beg you to embark, will not have been in vain. Your life will no doubt from then on find its own paths. That they will be good ones and rich and expansive — that I wish for you more than I can say.

What else shall I tell you? It seems to me everything has been said, with just the right emphasis. I wanted only to advise you to progress quietly and seriously in your evolvement. You could greatly interfere with that process if you look outward and expect to obtain answers from the outside — answers which only your innermost feeling in your quietest hour can perhaps give you.

I was very happy to find in your writing the

name of Professor Horaček. I harbor the highest regard for this kindest of scholars and owe him lasting gratitude. Would you please pass my sentiments on to him. It is very kind of him to think of me still, and I appreciate it.

I am returning the verses with which you entrusted me. I thank you again for your unconditional and sincere trust. I am overwhelmed with it, and therefore have tried, to the best of my ability, to make myself a little more worthy than I, as a stranger to you, really am.

With my sincerest interest and devotion,

Yours,

Rainer Maria Rilke

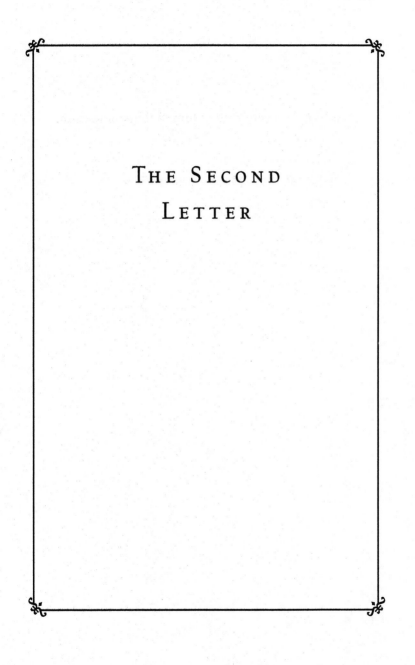

THE SECOND
LETTER

꧁

"We are unutterably alone, essentially,
especially in the things most intimate
and most important to us."

Viareggio, near Pisa, Italy
5 April 1903

You must forgive, my dear sir, that not until today could I gratefully turn my thoughts to your letter of February 24th. Until now I was not well, not exactly ill, but depressed by an influenza-type of fatigue. I was incapable of doing anything. Finally, when my situation did not seem to improve, I came to this southern seashore where I had been coaxed into well-being once before. But I am not well yet. Writing is difficult for me; therefore you must take these few lines to be more than they are.

Of course, you must know that you shall always

bring me joy with each of your letters. But please have forbearance with the answers, which may well often leave you empty-handed. We are unutterably alone, essentially, especially in the things most intimate and most important to us. In order for a person to advise, even to help another, a great deal must happen. Many different elements must coincide harmoniously; a whole constellation of things must come about for that to happen even once.

I wanted to tell you about two things today:

One is about irony: Do not allow it to control you, especially during uncreative moments. In creative moments allow it to serve you as another means to better understand life. If you use it with pure intent, then it is pure. One need not be ashamed of it. But beware of a viewpoint that is too consistently ironic; turn your attention to lofty and serious issues instead. In their presence irony will pale and become helpless. Scale the depths of things; irony will never descend there. And when you are exploring thus, and arrive at the brink of greatness, ask yourself whether this ironic attitude springs from a truly deep need of your being. For due to the impact of serious things, it will either fall away from you, if it is something merely incidental, or if it truly innately belongs to you, it will be strengthened to become an important tool, and take its place with all the other instruments with which you must build your own art.

The second thing that I wanted to tell you today is this:

Of all my books there are only a few that are indispensable to me. Two of them are constantly at my fingertips wherever I may be. They are here with me now: the Bible and the books of the great Danish writer, Jens Peter Jacobsen. I wonder whether you know his works. You can obtain them easily, for some of them are published in excellent translation. Do avail yourself of the small book *Six Stories* by J. P. Jacobsen and his novel *Niels Lyhne,* and begin with the first story in the first set, called "Mogens." A whole world will envelop you — the joy, the wealth, the incomprehensible greatness of a world! Live awhile within these books. Learn of them, whatever seems worth the learning, but above all, love them. For this love you shall be requited a thousand and a thousand times over, no matter what turn your life will take. This love, I am sure of it, will weave itself through the tapestry of your evolving being as one of the most important threads of your experiences, your disappointments, and your joys.

If I were obliged to tell you who taught me to

experience something of the essence of creativity, the depth of it and its enduring quality, there are only two names that I can name: that of *Jacobsen,* the very greatest of writers, and *Auguste Rodin,* the sculptor. No one among all artists living today compares with them.

Success in all your ways!

Yours,

Rainer Maria Rilke

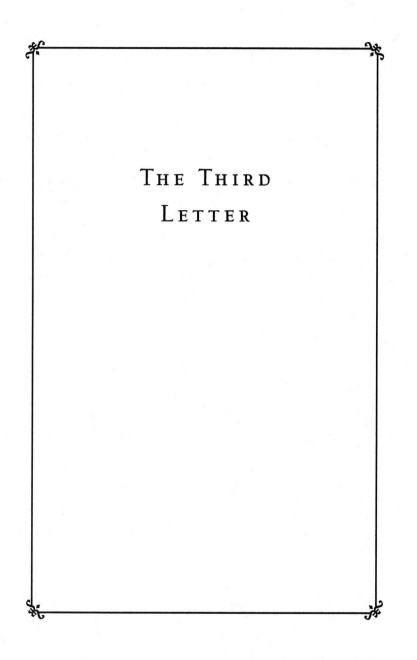

THE THIRD
LETTER

❦

*"Destiny itself is like a wonderful wide
tapestry in which every thread is guided
by an unspeakably tender hand, placed
beside another thread, and held and
carried by a hundred others."*

Viareggio, near Pisa, Italy
23 April 1903

You have brought me much joy, my dear sir, with your Easter letter, for it told me much good about you. The way in which you expressed yourself about Jacobsen's great and loving art showed me that I did not err in leading your life, with its many questions, to this treasure house.

Now *Niels Lyhne,* a book of grandeur and great depth, will reveal itself to you little by little, the more often you read it. It seems to contain everything, from life's most delicate fragrance to the most full-bodied flavor of its ripest and heaviest fruits. There is nothing in it that would not be understandable, comprehensible, or that would not ring true to experience. There is nothing in it that would not summon a familiar resonance echoing from the memory. No experience was too insignificant — the smallest happening unfolds like destiny. Destiny itself is like a wonderful wide tapestry in which every thread is guided by an unspeakably tender hand, placed beside another thread, and held and carried by a hundred others.

You will experience the greatest happiness reading this book for the first time and will move through its countless surprises as in a new dream. And as one goes through these books later, awestruck still, they lose nothing of their wonderful power nor relinquish any of their fairy tale quality with which they overwhelmed the reader the first time.

Only one becomes more and more delighted, more grateful, somehow clearer and simpler in one's perceptions. One has a deeper faith in life, is more content, and has somehow gained in self worth.

And later you must read the wonderful book about the fate and longing of *Marie Grubbe* and

Jacobsen's letters and journals and fragments, and finally, his poems. His poems live on, resounding in one's mind endlessly — even though they are only moderately well translated. In addition, I would advise you, when you have time, to buy the beautiful edition of the whole of Jacobsen's works. It contains all of these.

Concerning "Roses Should Be Standing Here..." — this work of incomparable eloquence and form — your negative opinion of the writer of the introduction is entirely and incontestably right. Let me ask you right here to read as little as possible of aesthetic critiques. They are either prejudiced views that have become petrified and senseless in their hardened lifeless state, or they are clever word games. Their views gain approval today but not tomorrow. Works of art can be described as having an essence of eternal solitude and an understanding is attainable least of all by critique. Only love can grasp and hold them and can judge them fairly. When considering analysis, discussion, or presentation, listen to your inner self and to your feelings every time. Should you be mistaken, after all, the natural growth of your inner life will guide you slowly and in good time to other conclusions. Allow your judgments their own quiet, undisturbed development, which, as with all progress, must come from deep within and can in no way be forced or hastened. *All things* consist of carrying to term and then giving birth. To allow the completion of every impression, every germ of a feeling deep within, in darkness, beyond words, in the realm of instinct unattainable by logic, to await humbly and patiently the hour of the descent of a new clarity: that alone is to live one's art, in the realm of understanding as in that of creativity.

In this there is no measuring with time. A year doesn't matter; ten years are nothing. To be an artist means not to compute or count; it means to ripen as the tree, which does not force its sap, but stands unshaken in the storms of spring with no fear that summer might not follow. It will come regardless. But it comes only to those who live as though eternity stretches before them, carefree, silent, and endless. I learn it daily, learn it with many pains, for which I am grateful: *Patience* is all!

࿊

My reaction to the books of Richard Dehmel — the same, by the way, as to the person, whom I do know slightly — is this: When I have found one of his well-written beautiful pages, I am then already afraid of the next ones, which destroy everything again and can turn that which is worthy of love into something unworthy. You have characterized him very well with the words, "lustful in his life and writing." Actually the creative experience lies so unbelievably close to the sexual, close to its pain and its pleasure, that both phenomena are only different forms of the same longing and bliss. If one could say "sexuality" instead of "lust" — sexuality in a large sense, in a wide pure sense, not one suspect by the church — then his art would be great and infinitely important. His poetic talent is great and as strong as the primeval urge; it has an impetuous rhythm that breaks forth out of him as water out of the rocks.

But it seems that this power of his is not always entirely genuine and not without assuming a pose. (After all, this is indeed one of the most difficult tests for the true artist: he must always remain innocently unaware of his best virtues if he does not wish to rob them of their spontaneity and their unaffectedness.) And when Dehmel's creative power, rushing through his being, meets the sexual, then it finds the man not quite so pure as he needs to be. For him there exists no totally mature and pure world of sex, none that is simply human and not *masculine* only. For him there exist lust, intoxication, and restlessness, beleaguered with the old prejudices and pride, with which the male has disfigured and burdened love. He loves only as *male*, not simply as a human being. Consequently there is in his perception something confining, something spiteful, seemingly wild, something temporal, not eternal. There is something that detracts from his art, and makes it suggestive and questionable. His art is not without blemish; it has been imprinted with passion and transience. Little of it will continue and endure. (But this is true of most art.)

In spite of that, one can appreciate and enjoy the part that is great. One must simply not be overwhelmed nor become a partisan to Dehmel's world, which is so infinitely fearful, full of adultery and confusion, far from the true destinies of man. They may on the one hand cause more real suffering than his fleeting gloom, but will also offer more opportunities for greatness and more courage for eternity.

Finally, regarding my books, I wish I could send you all of those that would somehow give you pleasure. However, I am very poor and my books, as soon as they are published, no longer belong to me. I can't even afford them myself, and, as I would often like, give them to those who would consider it a gift of love.

So I will write the titles and publishers of my most recent books on another piece of paper. (Of the newest ones published, there must be twelve or thirteen.) I must leave it up to you to order some of my works sometime at your convenience.

I am happy to know my books will be with you. Goodbye for now!

Yours,

Rainer Maria Rilke

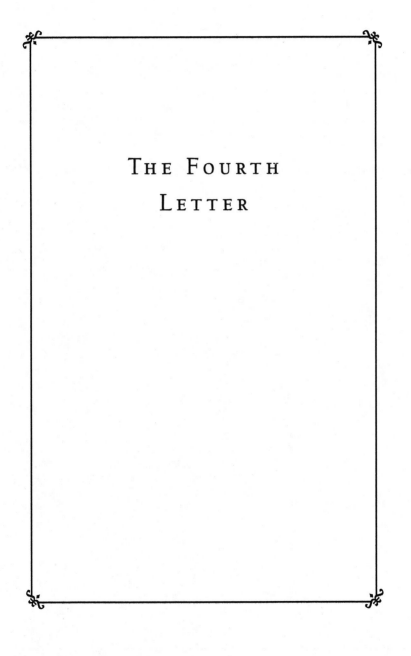

THE FOURTH
LETTER

꧁

*"If you will stay close to nature,
to its simplicity, to the small things hardly
noticeable, those things can unexpectedly
become great and immeasurable."*

Worpswede, near Bremen
16 July 1903

About ten days ago I left Paris, suffering and
tired, and rode into a large northern plain. Its
expanse, its quiet, and its sky are to restore my
health. But I entered the region during a long rain
that has not until today let up a bit over this restless
drifting land. I am using this first moment of
brightness to greet you, dear friend.

My dear Mr. Kappus, I have had a letter of yours
here for a long time, awaiting my answer. Not that I
had forgotten it; to the contrary, it is the kind that
one reads again, when one finds it among others. I

_ yours out to read, and you seemed so very near. It was the letter of May 2nd; you surely remember it. When I read it, as I am doing now, in the immense silence of this distant land, your beautiful concern about life touches me even more than it did in Paris, where everything seems strange, and one's impressions seem to tremble and fade into the terrible noise all around. Here, surrounded by a powerful land, over which the winds travel from the seas, here I feel that no man can answer those questions of yours and explain those feelings that in their depths have a life of their own. Even the best writers can err in their expressions when they are asked to interpret the faintest of impulses and that which is beyond words.

Nevertheless, I do believe you need not be left without answers, if you will cling to things resembling those that are now rejuvenating me. If you will stay close to nature, to its simplicity, to the small things hardly noticeable, those things can unexpectedly become great and immeasurable. If you will love what seems to be insignificant and will in an unassuming manner, as a servant, seek to win the confidence of what seems poor, then everything will become easier, more harmonious, and somehow more conciliatory, not for your intellect — that will most likely remain behind, astonished — but for your innermost consciousness, your awakeness, and your inner knowing.

You are so young; you stand before beginnings. I would like to beg of you, dear friend, as well as I can, to have patience with everything that remains unsolved in your heart. Try to love the *questions themselves,* like locked rooms and like books written in a foreign language. Do not now look for the answers. They cannot now be given to you because you could not live them. It is a question of experiencing everything. At present you need to *live* the question. Perhaps you will gradually, without even noticing it, find yourself experiencing the answer, some distant day. Perhaps you are indeed carrying within yourself the potential to visualize, to design, and to create for yourself an utterly satisfying, joyful, and pure lifestyle. Discipline yourself to attain it, but accept that which comes to you with deep trust, and as long as it comes from your own will, from your own inner need, accept it, and do not hate anything.

To cope with sexuality is difficult. Yes, but everything assigned to us is a challenge; nearly everything that matters is a challenge, and everything matters. If you would only recognize that and come to the place where you would strive on your own to finally gain your very own relationship with sexuality, always keeping aware of *your* native bent and *your* personality, your *own* experience, your childhood, and your strengths, then you need no longer fear losing yourself and becoming unworthy of your sexuality, your most precious possession.

Physical lust is a sensuous experience no different from innocently viewing something, or from the feeling of pure delight when a wonderful ripe fruit fills the tongue. It is a glorious infinite experience granted us, a gift of knowledge from the world, the fullness and radiance of all knowing. It is not bad that we welcome it. What is bad is that almost all misuse and waste it. They set it out as a lure in dreary places of their lives and use it as a distraction rather than as a focus on great heights.

Man has also transformed eating into something else. Lack on the one hand and excess on the other have clouded the clarity of this basic need. Similarly cloudy have become all the deep and simple human needs in which life renews itself. But the individual can clarify them for himself and can live that clarity — as long as he is not too dependent on others, as long as he has a pact with aloneness.

We can recall that all beauty in animals and

plants is a silent and enduring form of love and longing. We can see the animal just as we perceive the plant, patiently and willingly uniting, multiplying, and growing, not from physical desire, not from physical grief, rather from adapting to what has to be. That existing order transcends desire and grief and is mightier than will and resistance. The earth is full of this secret down to her smallest things. Oh, that we would only receive this secret more humbly, bear it more earnestly, endure it, and feel how awesomely difficult it is, rather than to take it lightly.

Oh, that we might hold in reverence our fertility, which is but *one*, even if it seems to be either spiritual or physical. Spiritual creativity originates from the physical. They are of the same essence — only spiritual creativity is a gentler, more blissful, and more enduring repetition of physical desire and satisfaction. The desire to be a creator, to give birth, to guide the growth process is nothing without its constant materialization in the world, nothing without the thousandfold consent of things and animals. Its enjoyment is so indescribably beautiful and rich only because it is filled with inherited memories of millions of instances of procreation and births. In one thought of procreation a thousand forgotten nights of love are resurrected and that thought is fulfilled in grandeur and sublimity. They who meet in the night to be entwined and sway in passionate lust are performing a serious work. They are gathering "sweets" and depth and power for the song of some future poet, who shall arise and speak of unspeakable bliss. They beg the future to wait to become the present, and they blindly embrace, believing their wish. Even so, they are mistaken. The future does come; a new human being arises, due to the law of nature. A strong resistant seed forces itself to the ovum that draws it willingly to itself.

Do not allow yourself to be misled by the surfaces of things. In the great depths all becomes law. They who live this mystery badly and ineffectually (and there are many), lose it only for themselves. Even so, they pass it on like a sealed letter without knowing it. Do not be misled by the great number of names and the complexity of cases. Perhaps there is over all a great motherhood expressed as mutual longing.

The beauty of a virgin, a being that, as you so aptly say, has not yet accomplished anything, is motherhood having a presentiment of itself, is in preparation, and has fears and longings. The beauty of the mother is that of a serving motherhood. And within the aged one there dwells an awesome memory.

Within the man, motherhood exists also, it seems to me, both physical and spiritual. His part in procreation is also a type of giving birth, and giving birth it is when he draws strength from his innermost abundance.

Perhaps the sexes are more closely related than one would think. Perhaps the great renewal of the world will consist of this, that man and woman, freed of all confused feelings and desires, shall no longer seek each other as opposites, but simply as members of a family and neighbors, and will unite as *human beings,* in order to simply, earnestly, patiently, and jointly bear the heavy responsibility of sexuality that has been entrusted to them.

But he who has a pact with aloneness can even now prepare the way for all of this that in the future may well be possible for many, and can build with hands less apt to err. Therefore, dear friend, embrace your solitude and love it. Endure the pain it causes, and try to sing out with it. For those near to you are distant, you say. That shows it is beginning to dawn around you; there is an expanse opening about you. And when your nearness becomes distant, then you have already expanded far: to being among the stars. Your horizon has widened greatly. Rejoice in your growth. No one can join you in that.

Be good to those who stay behind, and be quiet and confident in their presence. Do not torment them with your doubts, and do not shock them with your confidence or your joy, which they cannot understand. Try to establish with them a simple, sincere mutual feeling of communion, that need not change if you yourself change. Love the life that is theirs, although different from yours. Be considerate of aging persons, for they fear the very aloneness in which you place your trust. Avoid adding substance to those dramas always unleashed between parents and children. These encounters cause the children to expend much energy and consume the love of their elders. Even so, their love is warm, and has its effect, although it does not understand. Believe, however, in a love that will be safely kept for you as a legacy and a trust, and trust that in it there is a power and a blessing. You do not have to leave its presence in order to make very great strides ahead.

It is good that you are settling into a career that will make you independent, and that you will be relying completely on yourself in every sense. Wait patiently to see if your inner life feels restricted by the conditions of this career. I take it to be very difficult and very demanding, since it is burdened with many conventions, hardly allowing your personal interpretation of its designated duties. However, your pact with aloneness will be your support and solace even in the midst of unfamiliar situations. It is through that aloneness that you will find all your paths. All my wishes are prepared to accompany you, and so will my trust in you.

Yours,

Rainer Maria Rilke

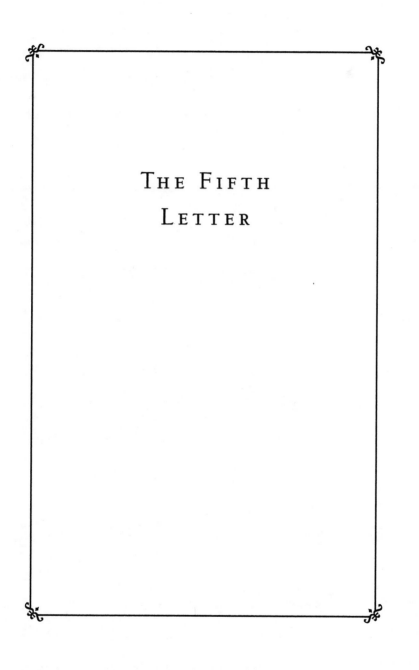

The Fifth
Letter

᪥

"There is much beauty here because
there is much beauty everywhere."

Rome
29 October 1903

My dear sir,

I received your letter of August 29th in Florence
and not until now, after two months, am I letting
you know it. Please excuse this belatedness. I do
dislike writing letters when traveling because I need
more than the basic writing implements: I need
quiet and solitude and at least one friendly hour.

We arrived in Rome about six weeks ago, at a
time when it was still empty, hot, and notoriously
feverish. This condition, along with other mundane
difficulties with accommodations, contributed to
the unrest around us that seemed not to want to
end, and to the strangeness of our surroundings

and our temporary homelessness. Rome, if one does not know the city, can be depressingly sad for the first few days. It affected me so, because it exudes a death-like, dreary atmosphere, typical of museums. The over-abundant relics of the past have been resurrected and their revival maintained with tremendous effort. From them a very small segment presently makes its living. All of these distorted and stale things are basically nothing more than coincidental remnants of another era and another kind of life, which is not ours and should not be considered as our own. They have been indiscriminately over-rated by many, including scholars and philologists and tourists, who habitually travel to Italy.

Finally, after weeks of daily resistance, one finds himself somewhat composed again, even if still a bit confused. One says to himself: No, there is not *more* beauty here than elsewhere. All these things have been restored and improved by the work of craftsmen. They have been and are admired and revered by generations past and present, and that will continue into the future. All these things mean nothing, are nothing, and have no heart, no worth. Yet there is much beauty here.

There is much beauty here because there is much beauty everywhere. Unending streams of lively water flow over the old aqueducts in the large city. They dance in the city squares over white stone bowls and spread themselves out in wide roomy basins. They rustle by day and raise their voice to the night. Night here is grand, expansive, soft from the winds, and full of stars. And gardens are here, unforgettable avenues lined with trees. And staircases are here, steps conceived by Michelangelo, steps that were modeled after downward gliding waters, broad in their descent, one step giving birth to another, as wave from wave. Through such impressions one composes himself and wins himself back from the demands of the multiplicities that speak and chatter. (How very talkative they are!) One gradually learns to recognize the very few things in which eternity dwells, which one can love, and solitude, of which one can softly partake.

I still reside in the city, at the Capitol, not far from the most beautiful sculpture of horse and rider that has been preserved for us from Roman art — that of Marcus Aurelius. However, in a few weeks I shall move to a quiet, modest room, an old summerhouse that lies lost deep in a large park, hidden from the noise and applause of the city. There I shall live the whole winter and shall enjoy the great silence. I expect it will give me the gift of pleasant times and hours of accomplishment. . . .

From there, where I shall feel more at home, I shall write you a longer letter and shall include the subject of your writing. Today I must tell you only this (perhaps it is not right that I did not do it sooner), that the book mentioned in your letter, which was to have contained work of yours, has not arrived here. Has it perhaps been returned to you, perhaps from Worpswede? For packages sent to a foreign country are not forwarded. This possibility is the most likely and I would appreciate a confirmation. I hope it does not mean a loss to you. I regret to say that in Italy this kind of situation is not unusual.

I would gladly have received this book, as is true of everything that pertains to you. Verses that you have meanwhile composed — if you entrust them to me — I shall always read, reread, and experience as well and as sincerely as I can.

With best wishes and greetings,

Yours,

Rainer Maria Rilke

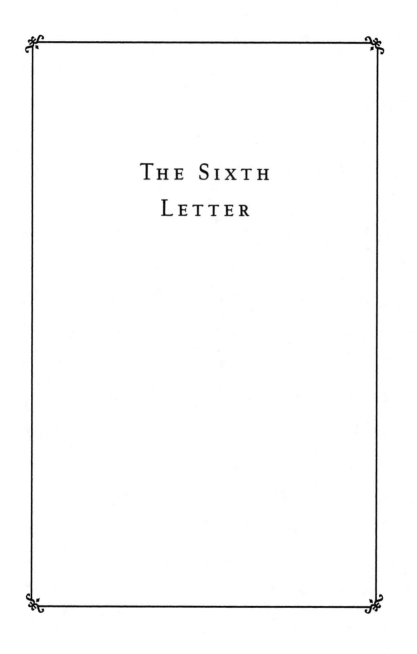

THE SIXTH
LETTER

❦

"Reflect on the world that you
carry within yourself.
And name this thinking what you wish. . . .
Your innermost happening is worth
all your love."

Rome
23 December 1903

My dear Mr. Kappus,

You should not be without a greeting from me at Christmastime, when in the midst of the festivities your feeling of aloneness is apt to weigh more heavily upon you. Whenever you notice that it looms large, then be glad about it. For what would aloneness be, you ask yourself, if it did not possess greatness? There exists only *one* aloneness, and it is *great,* and it is not easy to bear. To nearly everyone come those hours that we would gladly exchange for any cheap or even the most banal camaraderie, for even the slightest inclination to choose the second-best or the most unworthy thing. But perhaps it is exactly in those hours when aloneness can flourish. Its growth is painful as the growing up of a young boy and sad as the emergence of springtime.

But that should not confuse you. What you really need is simply this — aloneness, great inner solitude. To go within and for hours not to meet anyone — that is what one needs to attain. To be lonely as one was lonely as a child, while adults were moving about, entangled with things that seemed big and important, because the grownups looked so busy and because one could not understand any of their doings — that must be the goal. And when you realize one day that their activities are superficial, that their careers are paralyzed and no longer linked with life, then why not look at the world as a child would see it — out of the depths of your own world, out of the breadth of your own aloneness, which is itself work and rank and career? Why should anyone wish to exchange a child's wise incomprehension for resistance and disdain, since the incomprehension *is* aloneness, and resistance and disdain are an involvement in the things you seek to escape from.

Think, dear friend, reflect on the world that you

carry within yourself. And name this thinking what you wish. It might be recollections of your childhood or yearning for your own future. Just be sure that you observe carefully what wells up within you and place that above everything that you notice around you. Your innermost happening is worth all your love. You must somehow work on that.

Do not expend too much courage or time to clarify your position to others. I know your career is difficult and I anticipated your complaint and knew it would come. Now that it has come, I cannot reassure you. I can only advise you to think seriously about this: Are not all careers the same, filled with demands and people filled with animosity toward the individual, at the same time absorbing the hatred of those who have silently and sullenly adapted to dull duty? The situation that you are now obliged to tolerate is not burdened any heavier with conventions, prejudices, and errors than any other situation. If there are some who outwardly give the impression of granting more freedom, know that there really exists none that is related to the important things that make up real life. The individual person who senses his aloneness, and only he, is like a thing subject to the deep laws, the cosmic laws. If a person goes out into the dawn or gazes out into the evening filled with happenings, if he senses what happens there, then all situations fall away from him as from someone dead, even though he stands in the midst of life.

You, dear Mr. Kappus, as an officer in the military, need to experience this feeling. You must realize that you would have felt the same way in any existing career now. Yes, aside from that, independent of career, if you had sought connections in society, you would not have been spared this feeling of constraint. It is the same everywhere, but that is not a reason for fear or sadness. If there seems to be no communication between you and the people around you, try to draw close to those things that will not ever leave you. The nights are still there and the winds that roam through the trees and over many lands. Amidst things and among animals are happenings in which *you* can participate. The children too, are still the same as you were as a child, sad and happy in the same way. And if you think about your childhood, then you can again live among them, the lonely children — where the adults count for nothing and their dignity has no worth.

And if it is distressing and agonizing for you to think of your childhood and of the simplicity and silence so close akin to it, because you no longer believe in God, who is constantly appearing there, then ask yourself, dear Mr. Kappus, whether you have really lost God. Is it not rather true that you have not yet possessed him? For when could that have been? Do you think a child can hold him, him whom men can bear only with great effort and whose weight crushes the aged ones? Do you think that the one possessing him could lose him like a little stone? Or do you not rather agree that he who might have him could be lost *by him*? However, if you conclude that he did not exist in your childhood and not before that, if you surmise that Christ was deluded by his yearning and that Mohammed was betrayed by his pride — and if you, with great dismay, feel that he does not exist, even during this hour, while we are speaking of him, what right have you then to miss him, like someone out of the past, him, who never existed, and to seek him as though he were lost?

Why don't you think of him as the coming one, who has been at hand since eternity, the future one, the final fruit of a tree, with us as its leaves? What is keeping you from hurling his birth into evolving times and from living your life as though it were one painful beautiful day in the history of a great pregnancy? Don't you see that everything that happens becomes a beginning again and again? Could it not be *his* beginning, since a beginning in itself is always so beautiful? If, however, he is the most perfect one, would not what is less than perfect have to precede him, so that he can choose himself from great abundance? Would not *he* have to be the last one, in order to envelop everything within himself? And what sense would our existence make, if the one we longed for had already had his existence in the past?

By extracting the most possible sweetness out of everything, just as the bees gather honey, we thus build him. With any insignificant thing, even with the very smallest thing — if only it is done out of love — we begin, with work, with a time of rest following, with keeping silent or with a small lonely joy, with everything that we do alone, without participants or supporters, we begin him: the one whom we shall not experience in this lifetime, even as our ancestors could not experience us. Yet they who belong to the distant past are in us, serving as impetus, as a burden to our fate, as blood that can be heard rushing, as a gesture rising out of the depths of time.

Is there anything now that can rob you of the hope of someday being in him, who is the ultimate, in the infinite future, as once he was in your past?

Celebrate Christmas, dear Mr. Kappus, with this *reverent* feeling that he perhaps needs exactly this, your fear of life, in order to begin. Perhaps these very days of your transition are the times that he is touched by everything within you. Perhaps you are influencing him, just as you as a child with breathless effort left your mark on him. Be patient and without rancor and believe that the least we can do is to make his evolving no more difficult than the earth does for spring, when it wishes to come.

Be glad and comforted,

Yours,

Rainer Maria Rilke

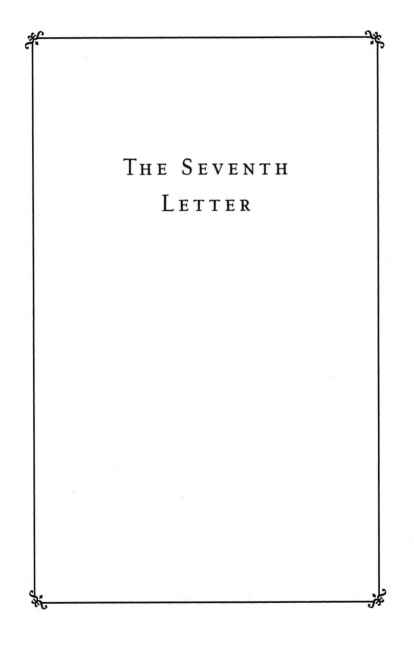

THE SEVENTH
LETTER

"We must embrace struggle.
Every living thing conforms to it.
Everything in nature grows and struggles
in its own way, establishing its own identity,
insisting on it at all cost, against all resistance."

Rome
14 May 1904

My dear Mr. Kappus,

Much time has elapsed since I received your last letter. Do not hold it against me. First it was work, then interruptions, and finally illness that over and over again kept me from responding. I did so wish it to come out of quiet and good days. Now I feel a bit better. The beginning of spring with its nasty and changeable moods was present here too, unmistakably so. And now I am finally able to greet you (which I do so very gladly) and to respond with one thing and another to your letter, as well as I can.

I have copied your sonnet because I found it beautiful and simple and well suited to the form in which it moves so naturally, with quiet proper decorum. It is the best of your verses that I have had the privilege to read. And now I shall give you my copy of them, for I know that it is important and also a new experience to find one's own work again in someone else's handwriting. Read these verses as though you had never seen them before, and you will feel in your innermost being how very much they are your own.

It was a joy for me to read this sonnet and your letter often. I thank you for both.

Do not allow yourself to be confused in your aloneness by the something within you that wishes to be released from it. This very wish, if you will calmly and deliberately use it as a tool, will help to expand your solitude into far distant realms. People have, with the help of so many conventions, resolved everything the easy way, on the easiest side of easy. But it is clear that we must embrace struggle. Every living thing conforms to it. Everything in nature grows and struggles in its own way, establishing its own identity, insisting on it at all cost, against all resistance. We can be sure of very little, but the need to court struggle is a surety that will not leave us. It is good to be lonely, for being alone is not easy. The fact that something is difficult must be one more reason to do it.

To love is also good, for love is difficult. For one human being to love another is perhaps the most difficult task of all, the epitome, the ultimate test. It is that striving for which all other striving is merely preparation. For that reason young people — who are beginners in everything — cannot yet love; they do not know how to love. They must learn it. With their whole being, with all strengths enveloping their lonely, disquieted heart, they must learn to love — even while their heartbeat is quickening. However, the process of learning always involves time set aside for solitude. Thus to love constantly and far into a lifespan is indeed aloneness, heightened and deepened aloneness for one who loves.

Love does not at first have anything to do with arousal, surrender, and uniting with another being — for what union can be built upon uncertainty, immaturity, and lack of coherence? Love is a high inducement for individuals to ripen, to strive to mature in the inner self, to manifest maturity in the outer world, to become that manifestation for the sake of another. This is a great, demanding task; it calls one to expand one's horizon greatly. Only in this sense, as the task to work on themselves, day and night, and to listen, ought young people use the love granted them. Opening one's self, and surrendering, and every kind of communion are not for them yet; they must for a very, very long time gather and harbor experience. It is the final goal, perhaps one which human beings as yet hardly ever seek to attain.

Young people often err, and that intensely so, in this way, since it is their nature to be impatient: They throw themselves at each other when love comes upon them. They fragment themselves, just as they are, in all of their disarray and confusion. But what is to follow? What should fate do if this takes root, this heap of half-broken things that they call togetherness and that they would like to call their happiness?

What of their future? Everyone loses himself for the sake of the other and loses the other and many others that would yet have wished to come. They lose perspective and limit opportunities. They exchange the softly advancing and retreating of gentle premonitions of the spirit for an unfruitful restlessness. Nothing can come of it; nothing, that is, but disappointment, poverty, and escape into one of the many conventions that have been put up in great numbers, like public shelters, on this most dangerous road. No area of human experience is provided with as many conventions as this one: there are flotation devices of the most unusual sort; there are boats and life belts. Society has known how to create every kind of refuge conceivable. Since it is inclined to perceive love life as entertainment, it needs to display it as easily available, inexpensive, safe, and reliable, just like common public entertainment.

It is true that many young people who do not love rightly, who simply surrender themselves and leave no room for aloneness, experience the depressing feeling of failure. They would, in their own personal way, like to turn the condition in which they find themselves into something meaningful and fruitful. Their nature tells them that questions of love can be solved even less easily than everything else usually considered important, and certainly not publicly or by this or that agreement. Questions of love are personal, intimate questions, from one person to another, that in every case require a new, a special, and an *exclusively* personal answer. But then, having already thrown themselves together, having set no boundaries between each other, and being no longer able to differentiate, they no longer possess anything of their own. How can they on their own find the escape route that they have already blocked to that inner solitude?

They act from a source of mutual helplessness. If, with the best of intentions, they wish to avoid the convention that is approaching them (marriage, for example) they find themselves in the clutches of another conventional solution, one less obvious, but just as deadly. Everything surrounding them, spread wide about them, is — convention. There, where a dull mutuality, prematurely established, is the basis for living, *every* action is conventional. Every situation leading to such confusion has its convention, be it ever so unusual, that is, in the ordinary sense, immoral. Yes, even separation would be a conventional step, an impersonal, coincidental decision, a weak and fruitless decision. Whoever will seriously consider the question of love will find that, as with the question of death, difficult as it is, there is no enlightened answer, no solution, not the hint of a path has yet been found. And for these two deep concerns that we carry safely disguised within us and that we pass on unresolved, for them no comforting principle will be learned, none finding general agreement.

But to the same degree that we as individuals

begin to explore life, to that degree shall these deep things surface for each of us in greater intimacy. The responsibility that the difficult work of love demands of our evolvement overwhelms us; it is larger than life. We, as yet beginners, are not equal to it. If we persevere after all, and take this love upon us, accepting it as a burden and a time of training, instead of losing ourselves to the frivolous and careless game behind which people have hidden themselves, not willing to face the most serious question of their being — then perhaps shall a small bit of progress be perceptible as well as some relief for those to come after us. That would be a great deal.

We are just now reaching the point where we can observe objectively and without judgment the relationship of one individual to a second one. Our attempts to live such a relationship are without a model. Yet, there already exist within our time frame some things intended to help our faint-hearted beginner's steps. The girl and the woman in their own new unfolding will only temporarily be imitators of male incivilities, of men's ways, and repeaters of men's careers. After the insecurity of this transition has passed, it will be shown that women, through their wealth of (often ridiculous) disguises and many changes, have continued their quest only in order to purify their own beings of the distorting influences of the other sex. The woman, within whom life dwells in a more direct, fruitful, and trusting way, must, after all, have become basically more mature, more human than the man. For he is easily pulled down by the weight of the lack of physical fruitfulness, pulled down under the surface of life; he professes to love that which he arrogantly and rashly underrates.

The simple humanity of woman, brought about through pain and abasement, shall then come to light when the convention of her ultra-feminism will have been stripped off, transforming her status in the world. The men, who today cannot yet feel it coming, shall be surprised and defeated by it. One day (in northern countries trustworthy signs can already be seen and heard), the girl and the woman shall exist with her name no longer contrasted to the masculine; it shall have a meaning in itself. It shall not bring to mind complement or limitation — only life and being: the feminine human being.

This progress shall transform the experience of love, presently full of error, opposed at first by men, who have been overtaken in their progress by women. It shall thoroughly change the love experience to the rebuilding of a relationship meant to be between two persons, no longer just between man and woman. And this more human love will be consummated, endlessly considerate and gentle, good and clear in its bonding and releasing; it shall resemble that love for which we must prepare painstakingly and with fervor, which will be comprised of two lonelinesses protecting one another, setting limits, and acknowledging one another.

And one more thing: Do not believe that this idea of a great love, which, when you were a boy, was imposed upon you, has been lost. Can you not say that since then great and good wishes have ripened within you, and resolutions too, by which you live today? I believe that this idea of love remains so strong and mighty in your memory because it was your first deep experience of aloneness and the first inner work that you have done on your life.

All good wishes for you, dear Mr. Kappus.

Yours,

Rainer Maria Rilke

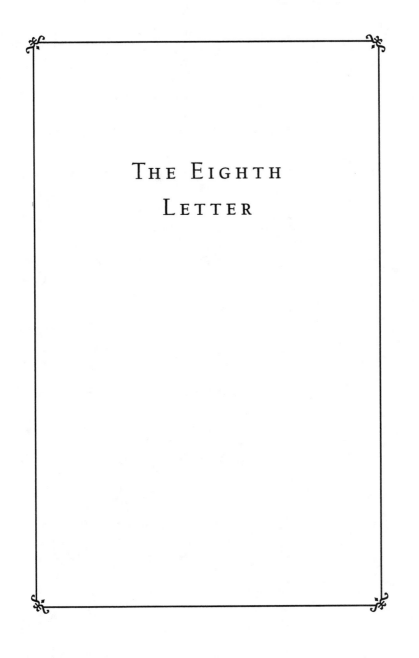

THE EIGHTH
LETTER

"How could we be capable of forgetting
the old myths that stand at the threshold
of all mankind, myths of dragons transforming
themselves at the last moment into princesses?
Perhaps all dragons in our lives are really
princesses just waiting to see us just once
being beautiful and courageous."

Borgeby gård, Flädie, Sweden
12 August 1904

I want to talk to you again for a little while, dear Mr. Kappus, even though I have hardly anything helpful to say — hardly anything useful. You have encountered many very sad experiences, which by now have passed. You say that even their passing was difficult and depressing. Please, dear friend, think about this: Did not this great sadness rather pass through you? Did not much within you change? Did you not, somehow at some place in your being, change while you were sad? The only sad experiences which are dangerous and bad are those that one reveals to people in order to drown them out. Like illnesses treated superficially and incompetently, they retreat and, after a short pause, break out even more intensely. They gather together within the self and are life. They are life unlived, ridiculed and scorned.

Were it possible, we might look beyond the reach of our knowing and yet a bit further into the past across the farmsteads of our ancestors. Then perhaps we would endure our griefs with even greater trust than our joys. For they are the moments when something new has entered into us, something unfamiliar. Our feelings become mute in timid shyness. Everything within us steps back; a silence ensues, and the something new, known to no one, stands in the center and is silent.

I believe that nearly all our griefs are moments of tension. We perceive them as crippling because we no longer hear signs of life from our estranged emotions. We are alone with the strange thing that has stepped into our presence. For a moment everything intimate and familiar has been taken from us. We stand in the midst of a transition, where we cannot remain standing.

And this is the reason the sadness passes: the something new within us, the thing that has joined us, has entered our heart, has gone into its inner-most chamber and is no longer there either — it is already in the blood. And we do not find out what it was. One could easily make us believe that nothing happened; and yet we have been changed, as a house is changed when a guest has entered it. We cannot say who came; we shall perhaps never know. But many signals affirm that the future has stepped into us in such a way as to change itself into us, and that long before it manifests itself outwardly.

Therefore it is so important to be alone and observant when one is sad. The seemingly unevent-ful moment, when our future really enters in, is very much closer to reality than that other loud and for-tuitous point in time, when it happens as if coming from the outside. The quieter and more patient, the more open we are when we are sad, the more res-olutely does that something new enter into us, the deeper it is absorbed in us, the more certain we are to secure it, and the more certain it is to become our *personal* destiny. When it "happens" at a later time — when it becomes obvious to others — then we feel an intimate kinship with it. And that is necessary. It is needed, and our evolvement will gradually go in that direction: nothing strange shall befall us, but rather that which has already for a long time belonged to us.

We have already had to rethink so many concepts about movement. Surely it is possible that we shall gradually learn to recognize that what we call fate emerges *from* human beings; it does not enter into them from the outside. It is only because so many did not absorb their destinies while they lived in them, did not transform them into themselves, that they did not recognize what emerged from them. Their fate was so strange to them that in their confused fright they believed it must just now have entered into them. For they swore never before to have found anything similar within themselves. As people were mistaken so long about the movement of the sun, so it is that people are yet mistaken about the movement of what is to come. The future stands firm and still, my dear Franz, but we are moving in infinite space.

Why should we not encounter difficulties?

To return to the subject of aloneness: It becomes increasingly clear that it is basically not something we can choose to have or not to have. We simply *are* alone. One can only delude one's self and act as though it were not so — that is all. How much better, however, that we concede we are solitary beings; yes, that we assume it to be true. Our minds will certainly reel at the thought, for all points on which we could heretofore focus shall be taken from us. There is nothing near and familiar left us; everything is in the distance, unendingly far away.

A person would have a similar feeling, were he, with practically no preparation or transition, taken from his home and placed on the summit of a high mountain. It would be a feeling of unequaled uncertainty — a vulnerability to a nameless something would nearly destroy him. He would think he were falling or would believe himself flung out into space or burst asunder into a thousand pieces. What a colossal lie his mind would have to invent to catch up with the condition of his senses and to clarify it. That is how all sense of distance, all measurements change for the one who is alone.

Some of these changes cause many to lose all perspective. And, as with the man on the pinnacle of the mountain, unusual imaginings emerge and strange sensations arise that seem to grow beyond everything endurable. But it is necessary that we experience *that* also. We must accept our existence *to the greatest extent possible;* everything, the unprecendented also, needs to be accepted. That is basically the only case of courage required of us: to be courageous in the face of the strangest, the most whimsical and unexplainable thing that we could encounter.

The fact that people have been cowards in that regard has caused infinite harm to life. The experiences that one calls "ghosts," the entire spirit world, death, all these related things have been forced out of life through daily resistance to such an extent that the senses with which we could grasp them have become atrophied. And that is not even considering the question of God.

The fear of the unexplainable not only impoverished the existence of the individual, but also caused the relationship of one person to another to be limited. It is as though fear has caused something to be lifted out of the riverbed of limitless possibilities to a fallow stretch of shore where nothing happens. For it is not inertia alone that causes the unspeakably monotonous and unrenewed human condition to repeat itself again and again. It is the aversion to anything new, any unpredictable experience, which is believed to be untenable.

Only he who can expect anything, who does not

exclude even the mysterious, will have a relationship to life greater than just being alive; he will exhaust his own wellspring of being. If we liken the existence of the individual to a room of larger or smaller size, it is evident that most people are familiar with only a corner of their room, perhaps a window seat or space where they pace to and fro. In that way they have a certain security. Yet every uncertainty fraught with danger is so much more human. It is the same uncertainty that motivated the prisoners in Edgar Allen Poe's stories to explore the form of their terrible prisons and not to be a stranger to the unspeakable horrors of their presence there.

But we are not prisoners. There are no traps or snares set for us, and there is nothing that should frighten or torture us. We are placed into life, into the element best suited to it. Besides, through thousands of years of adaptation, we have acquired such a resemblance to this life, that we, if we stood still, would hardly be distinguishable from our surroundings. We have no reason to mistrust our world, for it is not against us. If it has terrors, they are *our own* terrors. If it has precipices, they belong to us. If dangers are present, we must try to love them. And if we fashion our life according to that principle, which advises us to embrace that which is difficult, then that which appears to us to be the very strangest will become the most worthy of our trust, and the truest.

How could we be capable of forgetting the old myths that stand at the threshold of all mankind, myths of dragons transforming themselves at the last moment into princesses? Perhaps all dragons in our lives are really princesses just waiting to see us just once being beautiful and courageous. Perhaps everything fearful is basically helplessness that seeks our help.

You must not be frightened, dear Mr. Kappus, when a sadness arises within you of such magnitude as you have never experienced, or when a restlessness overshadows all you do, like light and the shadow of clouds gliding over your hand. You must believe that something is happening to you, that life has not forgotten you, that it holds you in its hand. It shall not let you fall.

Why should you want to exclude any anxiety, any grief, any melancholy from your life, since you do not know what it is that these conditions are accomplishing in you? Why do you want to persecute yourself with the question of where everything comes from and where it is headed?

You do know that you are in a period of transition and wish for nothing as much as to transform yourself. If some aspect of your life is not well, then consider the illness to be the means for an organism to free itself from something foreign to it. In that case you must help it to be ill and to have its whole illness, to let it break out. That is the course of its progress.

So much is happening within you at present, dear Mr. Kappus. You need to be as patient as someone ill and as optimistic as one recuperating, for perhaps you are both. And more: You are also the physician who must watch over yourself. But in the course of every illness there are many days in which the physician can do nothing but wait. And that, above all, to the extent that you are your physician, you must do now.

Do not scrutinize yourself too closely. Do not draw conclusions too quickly from that which is happening to you. Just allow it to happen. Otherwise you might easily begin to look with blame (that is, morally speaking) upon your past, which, of course, is very much a part of everything that you encounter now. The influences of the vagaries, the wishes and the longings of your boyhood upon your present life are not the ones you remember or pass judgment on. The unusual conditions of a lonely and helpless childhood are so difficult, so complicated, vulnerable to so many influences, and at the same time so distant from all real connections with life, that, whenever a vice may have entered, one may not simply call it a vice. One must, in any case, be very careful with that nomenclature. It is often the *name* of the crime upon which a life shatters, not the nameless and personal act itself at all. It might have been a definite necessity of this person's life, of which he may simply have availed himself.

The expending of effort seems so important to you only because you value victory too much. It is not the "great thing" that you believe to have achieved, even though you have a right to your feelings. The great thing is that there was something already present — and you were allowed to substitute it in place of your misconceptions — something true and real. Without it your victory also would have been a mere moral reaction without meaning. As it is, it has become a chapter in your life — your life, dear Mr. Kappus, I think of it with so many wishes for you.

Do you recall, from your childhood on, how very much this life of yours has longed for greatness? I see it now, how from the vantage point of greatness it longs for even greater greatness. That is why it does not let up being difficult, but that is also why it will not cease to grow.

If I were to tell you one more thing, it would be this: Do not believe that the one who seeks to comfort you lives without difficulty the simple and humble words that sometimes help you. His life contains much grief and sadness and he remains far behind you. Were it not so, he would not have found those words.

Yours,

Rainer Maria Rilke

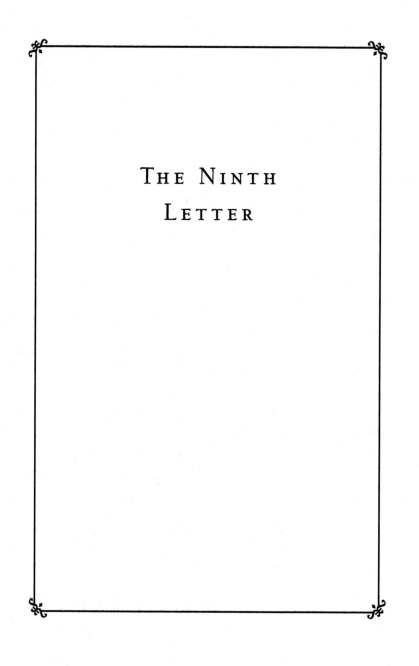

THE NINTH
LETTER

꧁

*"It is always my wish that you might find
enough patience within yourself to endure,
and enough innocence to have faith. . . .
Believe me, life is right in all cases."*

Furuborg, Jonsered, Sweden
4 November 1904

My dear Mr. Kappus,

During this time that has passed without a letter to you, I was traveling part of the time and partly so busy that I could not write. Even today writing is difficult, for before I could write your letter, I was obliged to write many others, so that my hand is tired. If dictating were possible, I would tell you so much. Instead, please accept just a few words as response to your long letter.

I think of you often, dear Mr. Kappus, and send you wishes with such concentration, that that itself should somehow help you. I am often in doubt that my letters can really be a help to you. Please don't answer with: Yes, they are! Just accept them without thanks and let us await what will happen.

It is probably not necessary to reply in detail to your letter. For what I could say to you about your inclination to doubt or about your inability to bring your inner and outer life into harmony, or about everything else that causes you concern — it is always that which I have already said: It is always my wish that you might find enough patience within yourself to endure, and enough innocence to have faith. It is my wish that you might gain more and more trust in whatever is difficult for you, in your aloneness, among other things. Allow life to happen to you. Believe me, life is right in all cases.

And about feelings: All feelings that integrate and inspire are pure. Impure is the feeling that touches only *one* side of your being and is tearing you up so. Everything you can think about in your childhood is good. Everything that causes you to be more than you have been in your best hours is right. Every advancement is good if it pervades your whole bloodstream, when it is not due to intoxication, not due to being conditioned to sadness, but to transparent joy. Do you understand what I mean?

Your doubt can become a good attribute if you *discipline* it. It must become a *knowing;* it must become the critic. Ask it, as often as it wishes to spoil something, why something is ugly. Demand proof of it, test it, and you will find it perhaps perplexed and confused, perhaps also in protest. But don't give in; demand arguments. Act with alertness and responsibility, each and every time, and the day will come when doubt will change from a destroyer to become one of your best fellow-workers, perhaps the wisest of all that have a part in building your life. That is all, dear Mr. Kappus, that I am able to say to you today. I shall under separate cover send you a small work that has appeared in Prague in the *Deutsche Arbeit.* In it I speak further to you of life and death and of how both are great and wonderful.

Yours,

Rainer Maria Rilke

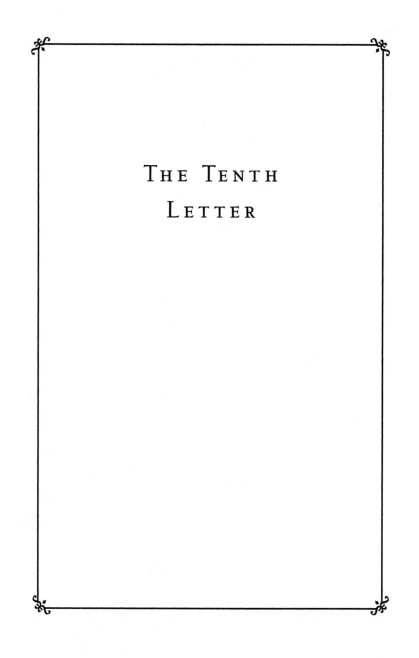

THE TENTH
LETTER

❦

"I can only wish that you trustingly and
patiently allow that grand solitude to work in
you. . . . It will act as an anonymous influence,
akin to how ancestral blood constantly moves
and merges with our own and links with that
of the individual, never to be unlinked."

Paris
the day after Christmas, 1908

You should know, dear Franz, how happy I was
to have received this beautiful letter of yours. The
messages that you sent me, sincere and frankly
expressed as they are again, were good news to me.
The longer I thought about it, the more I felt them
to be really good. I actually wanted to write this so
that you could receive it by Christmas Eve; but
because of the amount and variety of work with
which I am living uninterruptedly this winter, good

old Christmastime has approached so rapidly that I hardly had time to attend to the most necessary tasks, much less write. But I have thought of you often during these holidays and have imagined how tranquil you must be in your lonely fort between empty hills, attacked by great southern winds, as if they mean to devour them in large chunks.

The silence must be immense where there is space for such sound and movements. And when one realizes that the presence of the distant sea and its melody is added to all this, perhaps as the innermost tone in this prehistoric harmony, then I can only wish that you trustingly and patiently allow that grand solitude to work in you. It is no longer possible to be erased from your life. It shall be immanent in all that you experience and all that you do. It will act as an anonymous influence, akin to how ancestral blood constantly moves and merges with our own and links with that of the individual, never to be unlinked. It is gently decisive at each crossroad of our life.

Yes, I am glad that you now have this certain, steady, safe career existence. This title, this uniform, this military service — all of these tangible but restrictive things — in surroundings with a small staff equally isolated, take on a seriousness and an importance above the usual playfulness, the waiting-for-the-time-to-pass characteristic of the military career. This environment not only necessitates vigilance in application, and allows for independent attentiveness to detail, but it actually provides training for these qualities. To be in circumstances that work in us, that place us before great aspects of nature from time to time, that is all we need.

Art also is only a way of life, and we can, no matter how we live, and without knowing it, prepare ourselves for it. With each encounter with truth one draws nearer to reaching communion with it, more so than those in unreal, half-artistic careers — by pretending proximity to art, they actually deny and attack the existence of all art. All those in the field of journalism and nearly all critics do it, as well as three-fourths of those engaged in literature, or who wish to call it that. I am glad that you have overcome the danger of being caught up in such a realm, and that you are somewhere in a rugged reality alone and courageous.

May the year ahead of you keep and strengthen you in that resolve.

Always,

Yours,

Rainer Maria Rilke

About the Author

Rainer Maria Rilke was born in Prague, Czechoslovakia, in 1875. His father was an officer in the army, and he was at first sent to a military school. After that, largely on his own, he studied philosophy, history, literature, and art in Prague, Munich, and Berlin.

He started writing poetry at an early age, and became famous, first in Europe and then worldwide, for his poetry, novels, and letters. He traveled widely throughout Germany, Russia, France, Italy, Spain, Switzerland, Egypt, and Scandinavia.

He married Clara Westhoff in 1901, and had a daughter, Ruth, in 1902. After the birth of their daughter, they moved to Paris, where Clara worked with the famous sculptor Auguste Rodin, and Rilke wrote a monograph on him.

He died in France in 1926, and is buried beside the little church of Raron, overlooking the Rhone Valley.

About the Translator

Joan Marie Burnham was born in Berlin, Germany. She moved to Milwaukee, Wisconsin, at age ten and remained there until she graduated with honors from Milwaukee-Downer College (now Lawrence University) with majors in German and English.

Her postgraduate work consisted of study in Germany, where she earned a Master's Degree in Teaching of German from the University of Georgia.

She lives in Marin County, California.

POSSIBILITY OF BEING

A Selection of Poems by

Rainer Maria Rilke

Translated by J. B. Leishman

CONTENTS

THE BOOK OF HOURS
(1905)

WITH STROKES THAT RING CLEAR

With strokes that ring clear and metallic, the hour
to touch me bends down on its way:
my senses are quivering. I feel I've the power—
and I seize on the pliable day.

Not a thing was complete till by me it was eyed,
every kind of becoming stood still.
Now my glances are ripe and there comes like a bride
to each of them just what it will.

There's nothing so small but I love it and choose
to paint it gold-groundly and great
and hold it most precious and know not whose
soul it may liberate . . .

I LIVE IN EXPANDING RINGS

I live in expanding rings that are weaving
over these things below.
The last, perhaps, is beyond my achieving,
I'll make an attempt at it though.

Round God, the old tower, my gyres I perform,
and I've gyred there centuries long;
and don't know whether I'm falcon or storm
or, maybe, a mighty song.

WHAT WILL YOU DO, GOD?

What will you do, God, if Death takes me?
I am your jug (if someone breaks me?)
I am your drink (if curdling cakes me?)
I am your trim, your trade—it makes me
think: with me goes your meaning too.

You'll have no house to turn into,
where words, so near and warm, will greet then.
They'll fall from off your weary feet then,
those velvet sandals I'm for you.

Your cloak will slip from off your shoulders.
Your glance, which on my cheek would rest,
warmly as by a pillow pressed,
will come, and, after much vain quest,
sink, as the sun goes down the west,
into some lap of alien boulders.

What will you do, God? I'm distressed.

YOU MUSTN'T BE AFRAID, GOD

You mustn't be afraid, God. They say *mine*
to all those things whose patience does not fail.
They're like a gale against the branches blowing
and saying "*My* tree."

4

They scarcely see
how everything their hands can seize is glowing
so hot that even by its extremity
they could not hold it without getting burnt.

They say *mine,* as with peasants one will dare
to say "My friend the Prince" in conversation,
when that impressive prince is otherwhere.
They say *mine* of their alien habitation,
while knowing nothing of the master there.
They say *mine* and they speak of properties,
when everything upcloses which they near:
just as a mountebank might have no fear
of calling even sun and lightning his.
That's how they talk: "My life," they say, "My
        wife,"
"My dog," "My child," although they know that life
and wife and dog and child are all alike
remote configurings on which they strike
with outstretched hands in blind obscurity.
True, only great men know this certainly,
and long for eyes. The rest refuse to hear
that all their wretched wandering career
is with no single thing in harmony,
and that, rejected by their property,
owners disowned, they no more have the power
to own a woman than to own a flower,
which leads a life that's foreign to us all.

Ah, God, don't lose your balance. Even he
who loves you and in darkness still can see
and know your face, when like a wavering light
he feels your breath, does not possess you quite.
And if at night by some one you are guessed,
so that you're forced to come into his prayer:
      you're still the guest
      that onwardly will fare.

God, who can hold you? You are just your own,
whom no possessor's hand can be upsetting,
even as the still-maturing, sweeter-getting
vintage belongs but to itself alone.

THE BOOK OF IMAGES
(1902 and 1906)

GIRLS

Others on lengthy wanderings
to the darksome poets are forced to fare;
must always be asking a traveler
if he's not seen one singing there
or laying his hands on strings.
Only girls will never ask
what bridge leads to images;
will smile merely, brightlier than necklaces
of pearl against silver bowls unfurled.

All doors from their lives are entrances
into a poet
and into the world.

FROM A CHILDHOOD

Rich darkness round the room was streaming
where the boy sat, quite hidden in himself.
His mother came, a dream within his dreaming,
and a glass quivered on a silent shelf.
Feeling the room had given her away,
she kissed him—"So it's you"—and let him be . . .
Then both glanced at the piano timidly,
for often of an evening she would play,
and had a song that drew him deep and clung.

He sat there very still. His large gaze hung
upon her hand which, under bright rings bowing,
as though with labor through a snow-drift plowing,
over the white keys softly swung.

PONT DU CARROUSEL

That blind man standing by the parapet,
gray as some nameless empire's boundary stone,
he is perhaps that something unbeknown
to which the planetary clock is set,
the silent center of the starry ways;
for all around him strives and struts and strays.

He keeps his movelessly inerrant station
where manifold perplexing crossways go;
the somber entrance to the world below
among a superficial generation.

AUTUMN DAY

Lord, it is time. The summer was so great.
Impose upon the sundials now your shadows
and round the meadows let the winds rotate.

Command the last fruits to incarnadine;
vouchsafe, to urge them on into completeness,
yet two more south-like days; and that last
      sweetness,
inveigle it into the heavy vine.

He'll not build now, who has no house awaiting.
Who's now alone, for long will so remain:
sit late, read, write long letters, and again
return to restlessly perambulating
the avenues of parks when leaves downrain.

AUTUMN

The leaves are falling, falling as from far,
as though above were withering farthest gardens;
they fall with a denying attitude.

And night by night, down into solitude,
the heavy earth falls far from every star.

We are all falling. This hand's falling too—
all have this falling-sickness none withstands.

And yet there's One whose gently-holding hands
this universal falling can't fall through.

PRESENTIMENT

I'm like a flag surrounded by distance.
Divining the coming winds, I must share their
        existence,
whereof things below reveal as yet no traces:
doors are still closing softly and quiet are
        the fire-places;
windows are not yet shaking, and dust lies heavily.

But I can already sense the storm, and surge like
        the sea.
And spread myself out and into myself downfall
and hurtle myself away and am all
alone in the great storm.

THE VOICES

Nine Leaves with a Title-Leaf

TITLE-LEAF

The rich and fortunate need no mention,
what they are troubles no one's mind.
The needy, though, have to attract attention,
have to be saying: I am blind,
or else: that's what I soon shall be;
or: everything here goes wrong with me;
or: I've left an ailing child behind;
or: that's the place where I've been spliced . . .

And perhaps this hasn't at all sufficed.

And, since otherwise everyone just goes flinging
past them like wings, they have to be singing.

And there one still can hear good song.

People are odd; they'll travel farther
and hear a choir of *castrati* rather.

When tired of such choirs, though, to listen for long
to these voices comes God the Father.

THE BEGGAR'S SONG

From door to door in shower and shine
I pass continually;
into my right hand I consign
my right ear suddenly.
Then as something I never knew was mine
my voice will seem to me.

Then who is crying, whether it's I
or another, I'm not quite sure.
It's only a trifle for which I cry.
The poets cry for more.

And finally I shut my face
with both my eyes up tight;
as it lies with its weight in my hand's embrace
it's quite a restful sight.

13

Lest any should think I'd got no place
to lay my head at night.

THE BLIND MAN'S SONG

I'm blind, you outsiders, and that's an affliction,
that's an abhorrence, a contradiction,
something that daily exceeds me.
My hand upon my wife's arm I lay,
gray hand of mine upon her gray gray,
and through a sheer void she leads me.

You touch and push and imagine your own
sound differs from that of stone upon stone,
and yet you're mistaken: I alone
am living and suffering and sighing.
In me there's a never-ending cry—
it may be my heart or my bowels, but I
don't know which of them's crying.

If ever you sang these songs, no trace
was there of this inflection.
Warmly each day to your dwelling-place
comes a new sun's reflection.
And you've got a feeling of face-to-face,
and that makes for self-protection.

THE DRINKER'S SONG

It wasn't in me. In and out it would go.
I wanted to hold it. The wine held it, though.
(What it was, I no longer can say.)
Then the wine held this and the other thing out,
till I came to trust it beyond all doubt.
In my imbecile way.

Now I'm in its power, and it flings me at will
about and about and is losing me still
to Death, that son of a bitch.
If he wins me, dirty card that I am,
he'll use me to scratch his grisly ham
and toss me into the ditch.

THE SUICIDE'S SONG

Another moment to live through, then.
How the rope I fasten, again and again
someone cuts.
I'd got prepared so wonderfully,
and already a little eternity
was in my guts.

They bring me now, as they've done before,
this spoonful of life to sup.
No, I won't, I won't have any more,
let me bring it up.

Life's an excellent thing, I know,
through all the world outspread;
I simply can't digest it, though,
it only goes to my head.

It nourishes others, it makes me ill;
one *can* dislike the thing.
What for a thousand years I'll still
require is dieting.

THE WIDOW'S SONG

Life was kind to me at the start.
It kept me warm, it put me in heart.
That with all who are young it has that art,
how could I then be aware?
I didn't know what life could be—
it was nothing but years quite suddenly,
with no kindness or wonder or novelty,
as though torn in two pieces there.

That was neither its fault nor my own;
we both were left with patience alone,
but Death has not a whit.
I saw him coming (in what a way!),
and watched him taking and taking away:
I had no claim to it.

What was my own, mine really?
Was not even my misery
only a loan from Fate?

16

Fate doesn't merely want happiness,
but pain back as well and outscreamed distress,
and buys ruin at a second-hand rate.

Fate was there and obtained for a sou
every expression that came into
my face or away would glide.
A clearance sale was held each day,
and when I was empty it went away
and left me unoccupied.

THE IDIOT'S SONG

They don't interfere. They let me be.
They say that nothing can happen to me.
How good!
Nothing can happen. All comes to soar
round the Holy Spirit for evermore,
round that Spirit for ever sure—
how good!

No, one mustn't suppose there could ever begin
to be any kind of danger therein.
There is, to be sure, the blood.
The blood's the hardest, without a doubt.
I sometimes think I shall have to fall out—
(How good!)

Oh, what a lovely ball up there;
red and round as an everywhere.

Good, that you caused it to be.
Would it come if I called it to me?

All's behaving in such a remarkable way,
now drifting together, now swimming away:
friendly, a little hard to survey.
How good!

THE ORPHAN GIRL'S SONG

I'm no one, and no one is what I shall be.
I'm still too small to exist, I agree;
but I'll always be so.

Mothers and fathers, oh,
have pity on me.

Bringing up's not worth the pains, I'll allow:
I shan't escape my fate.
No one can need me: it's too soon now,
and tomorrow it's too late.

I've only got this dress you see,
growing thin and colorless;
bur perhaps it'll last an eternity
before God none the less.

I've only got this bit of hair
(the same as it was before),
which used to be someone's dearest care.

Nothing's dear to him any more.

THE DWARF'S SONG

My soul is straight and good maybe;
my heart, though, my blood flowing crookedly,
all that which so distresses me,
just can't hold it upright here.
It has no garden, it has no bed,
it clings to my sharp bones instead
and beats its wings with fright here.

My hands too will always be failing me.
How hopelessly stunted they are you can see:
damp, heavy, hopping constrictedly
like little toads in wet weather.
And everything else about me too
is old and worn and sad to view;
why does God delay to do
away with it altogether?

Is he angry with me for my face
with the mouth that seems to rue it?
It was often so ready to grow in grace
and let a light shine through it.
But of all that moved about the place
big dogs came closest to it.
And of that dogs have no trace.

THE LEPER'S SONG

Look, I am forsaken by everything.
Of me not one in the town knows anything,
I have become a leper.
And I rattle about with this rattle of mine,
knocking my melancholy sign
into the ears, to their dismay,
of every too-near-stepper.
And those that hear its woodenness, they
take good care not to look this way,
and won't learn what has happened here.

As far as my rattle's sound reaches, I
am at home; but perhaps the reason why
you make my rattle so loud is just
that my distance too may provoke mistrust
in those my nearness can terrify.
And thus for years on end I can,
without discovering maid or man,
woman or child, be faring.

Brutes I'll refrain from scaring.

NEW POEMS
(1907 and 1908)

EARLY APOLLO

As framing boughs, still leafless, can exhibit
a morning that's already all in Spring,
there's nothing in his head that could prohibit
the splendor of all poems from centering

upon us with an almost fatal shining;
for in his gaze as yet no shadow plays,
his temples are too cool for laurel's twining,
and from his eyebrows not till later days

will that tall-stemmed rose garden be uplifting,
and loosened petals, one by one, be drifting
along the tremors of the mouth below,

as yet still silent, sparkling and unused,
just drinking something with its smile, as though
its singing were being gradually infused.

LOVE-SONG

How shall I hold my soul, that it may not
be touching yours? How shall I lift it then
above you to where other things are waiting?
Ah, gladly would I lodge it, all-forgot,
with some lost thing the dark is isolating
on some remote and silent spot that, when
your depths vibrate, is not itself vibrating.

You and me—all that lights upon us, though,
brings us together like a fiddle-bow
drawing *one* voice from two strings it glides along.
Across what instrument have we been spanned?
And what violinist holds us in his hand?
O sweetest song.

EASTERN AUBADE

Does it not, though, like a coast appear,
a strip of coast, this bed on which we're lying?
Those lofty breasts of yours alone are clear
to my grown-dizzy feeling's dim descrying.

For, oh, this night in which so much was screaming,
in which beasts called and rent themselves in prey,
is it not grimly strange to us? And, gleaming
outside so slowly there and called the day,
is that too really more familiar-seeming?

One needs to be as much within another
as anthers are in petals: so unending
around us things immeasurably transcending
accumulate until they almost smother.

While, though, with these embraces we are keeping
unnoticed that in-closing enmity,
from you, from me, it still can be outleaping:
for, oh, our spirits live by treachery.

24

DAVID SINGS BEFORE SAUL

1

Can you hear, King, how my instrument
flings out distances through which we're wending?
Stars encounter us uncomprehending,
and at last like rain we are descending,
and a flowering follows that descent.

Girls you still were able to possess
flower from women tempting my defenses;
scent of virgins reassails your senses;
slender boys stand, all excitedness,
panting where some hidden stair commences.

Would my strings could bring back everything!
But my music's reeling drunkenly.
Ah, those nights of yours, those nights, my King—
and, grown heavier from your handselling,
how superb those bodies all could be!

I can match you their remembered splendor,
since I can divine it. How, though, render
for you their dark groans of ecstasy?

2

King, who had such blessings here below,
and who now with life that never ceases
overshadow me and overthrow:
come down from your throne and break in pieces
this my harp you are exhausting so.

Look, it's like an amputated tree:
through its boughs, where fruits for you were
        growing,
depths now, as of days to come, are showing—
scarcely recognizable by me.

Let me by its side no more be sleeping;
look, King, at this boyish hand: do you
really think it cannot yet be leaping
through the octaves of a body too?

3
Though you're hiding in the dark somewhere,
King, I have you still within my hold.
Look, my firm-spun song's without a tear,
and the space around us both grows cold.
My deserted heart and your untended
in your anger's clouds are both suspended,
madly bit into each other there
and into a single heart uprolled.

How we change each other, can you clearly
feel now? Burden's being inspirited.
If we hold to one another merely,
you to youth, King, I to age, we're nearly
like a star that's circling overhead.

THE DEPARTURE OF
THE PRODIGAL SON

Now to depart from all this incoherence
that's ours, but which we can't appropriate,
and, like old well-springs, mirrors our appearance
in trembling outlines that disintegrate;
from all this, that with bramble-like adherence
is once more clinging to us—to depart,
and then to start
bestowing on this and that you'd ceased to see
(so took for granted was their ministration)
a sudden gaze: all reconciliation,
tender and close and new-beginningly;
and to divine the whelming desolation,
the inexorable impersonality,
of all that childhood needed to withstand—
And even then depart, hand out of hand,
as though you tore a wound that had been healing,
and to depart: whither? To unrevealing
distance, to some warm, unrelated land,
that, back-clothwise, will stay, without all feeling,
behind all action: garden, sea or sand;
and to depart: why? Impulse, generation,
impatience, obscure hope, and desperation
not to be understood or understand:

To take on all this, and, in vain persistence,
let fall, perhaps what you have held, to die
alone and destitute, not knowing why—

Is this the way into some new existence?

27

THE OLIVE GARDEN

And still he climbed, and through the gray
    leaves thrust,
quite gray and lost in the gray olive lands,
and laid his burning forehead full of dust
deep in the dustiness of burning hands.

After all, this. And, this, then, was the end.
Now I'm to go, while I am going blind;
and, oh, why wilt Thou have me still contend
Thou art, whom I myself no longer find.

No more I find Thee. In myself no tone
of Thee; nor in the rest; nor in this stone.
I can find Thee no more. I am alone.

I am alone with all that human fate
I undertook through Thee to mitigate,
Thou who art not. Oh, shame too consummate . . .

An angel came, those afterwards relate.

Wherefore an angel? Oh, there came the night,
and turned the leaves of trees indifferently,
and the disciples stirred uneasily.
Wherefore an angel? Oh, there came the night.

The night that came requires no specifying;
just so a hundred nights go by,
while dogs are sleeping and while stones are lying—
just any melancholy night that, sighing,
lingers till morning mount the sky.

For angels never come to such men's prayers,
nor nights for them mix glory with their gloom.
Forsakenness is the self-loser's doom,
and such are absent from their father's cares
and disincluded from their mother's womb.

PIETÀ

So, Jesus, once again I am beholding
those feet that seemed so youthful to me there
when I unshod and washed them, greatly fearing;
oh, how they stood entangled in my hair,
like some white wild thing from a thorn-bush
    peering.

Those limbs, from every lover so withholding,
for the first time in this love-night I view.
We've never felt each other's arms enfolding,
and now I only weep and watch for you.

But, look, how torn your hands have come to be—
not from my bites, beloved, not by me.
Your heart stands open now for all to share:
I only should have had the entry there.

Now you are tired, and your tired mouth is urged
by no desire for my sad mouth, alas!—
O Jesus, Jesus, when did our time pass?
How strangely both of us are being submerged.

THE POET'S DEATH

He lay. His high-propped face could only peer
in pale refusal at the silent cover,
now that the world and all this knowledge of her,
torn from the senses of her lover,
had fallen back to the unfeeling year.

Those who had seen him living saw no trace
of his deep unity with all that passes;
for these, these valleys here, these meadow-grasses,
these streams of running water, *were* his face.

Oh yes, his face was this remotest distance,
that seeks him still and woos him in despair;
and his mere mask, timidly dying there,
tender and open, has no more consistence
than broken fruit corrupting in the air.

BUDDHA

As though he listened. Stillness: something far . . .
We hold our breath; our hearing though's too dim.
And he is star. And many a mighty star,
beyond our vision, is attending him.

Oh, he is all. Lingering, have we the least
hope that he'll notice? Could he ever need?

And if we fell before him here to plead,
he'd still sit deep and idle as a beast.

For that in him which drags us to his feet
has circled in him for a million years.
He who forgets our hopes and fears
in thoughts from which our thoughts retreat.

L'ANGE DU MÉRIDIEN

Chartres

In storm, that round the strong cathedral rages
like a denier thinking through and through,
your tender smiling suddenly engages
our hearts and lifts them up to you:

O smiling angel, sympathetic stone,
with mouth as from a hundred mouths distilled:
do you not mark how, from your ever-filled
sundial, our hours are gliding one by one—

that so impartial sundial, upon which
the day's whole sum is balanced equally,
as though all hours alike were ripe and rich?

What do you know, stone-nurtured, of our plight?
With face that's even blissfuller, maybe,
you hold your tables out into the night.

THE CATHEDRAL

In those small towns where, clustered round about,
old houses squat and jostle like a fair,
that's just caught sight of *it,* and then and there
shut up the stalls, and, silenced every shout,

the criers still, the drum-sticks all suspended,
stands gazing up at it with straining ears:
while it, as calm as ever, in the splendid
wrinkled buttress-mantle rears
itself above the homes it never knew:

in those small towns you come to realize
how the cathedrals utterly outgrew
their whole environment. Their birth and rise,
as our own life's too great proximity
will mount beyond our vision and our sense
of other happenings, took precedence
of all things; as though that were history,
piled up in their immeasurable masses
in petrification safe from circumstance,
not that, which down among the dark streets passes
and takes whatever name is given by chance
and goes in that, as children green or red,
or what the dealer has, wear in rotation.
For birth was here, within this deep foundation,
and strength and purpose in this aspiration,
and love, like bread and wine, was all around,
and porches full of lovers' lamentation.
In the tolled hours was heard life's hesitation,
and in those towers that, full of resignation,
ceased all at once from climbing, death was found.

THE ROSE WINDOW

In there: the lazy-pacing paws are making
a silence almost dizzying you; and then
how suddenly one cat-like creature's taking
the glance that strays to it and back again

into its great eye irresistibly—
the glance which, grasped as in a whirlpool's twist,
floats for a little while revolvingly
and then sinks down and ceases to exist,

when that eye, whose reposefulness but seems,
opens and closes with a raging clasp
and hales it in to where the red blood streams—

Thus from the darkness there in days gone by
would the cathedrals' great rose-windows grasp
a heart and hale it into God on high.

GOD IN THE MIDDLE AGES

And they'd got him in themselves upstored,
and they wanted him to reign forever,
and they hung on him (a last endeavor
to withhold his journey heavenward

and to have him near them in their slumbers)
their cathedrals' massive weights. He must
merely wheel across his boundless numbers
pointingly and, like a clock, adjust

what they daily toiled at or transacted.
But he suddenly got into gear,
and the people of the stricken town

left him—for his voice inspired such fear—
running with his striking-works extracted,
and absconded from his dial's frown.

THE PANTHER

Jardin des Plantes, Paris

His gaze those bars keep passing is so misted
with tiredness, it can take in nothing more.
He feels as though a thousand bars existed,
and no more world beyond them than before.

Those supply-powerful paddings, turning there
in tiniest of circles, well might be
the dance of forces round a center where
some mighty will stands paralyticly.

Just now and then the pupil's noiseless shutter
is lifted.—Then an image will indart,
down through the limbs' intensive stillness flutter,
and end its being in the heart.

THE GAZELLE

Gazella Dorcas

Enchanted thing: however can the chime
of two selected words attain the true
rhyme that, as beckoned, comes and goes in you?
Out of your forehead leaf and lyre climb,

and all you are has been in simile
passing through those love-songs continually
whose words will cover, light as leaves of rose,
the no-more-reader's eyes, which he will close:

only to look upon you: so impelled
as though each limb of yours with leaps were laden,
and held its fire but while the neck upheld

the head in hearkening: as when a maiden
breaks off from bathing in some lonely place,
the forest-lake within her swift-turned face.

THE UNICORN

And then the saint looked up, and in surprise
the prayer fell like a helmet from his head:
for softly neared that never-credited
white creature, which, like some unparented,
some helpless hind, beseeches with its eyes.

The ivory framework of the limbs so light
moved like a pair of balances deflected,
there glided through the coat a gleam of white,
and on the forehead, where the beams collected,
stood, like a moon-lit tower, the horn so bright,
at every footstep proudly re-erected.

Its mouth was slightly open, and a trace
of white through the soft down of grey and rose
(whitest of whites) came from the gleaming teeth;
its nostrils panted gently for repose.
Its gaze, though, checked by nothing here beneath,
projecting pictures into space,
brought a blue saga-cycle to a close.

THE DONOR

The painters' guild was given this commission.
His Lord, perhaps, he did not really see;
perhaps, as he was kneeling in submission,
no saintly bishop stood in this position
and laid his hand upon him silently.

To kneel like this was everything, maybe
(just as it's all that we ourselves have known):
to kneel: and hold with choking breath one's own
contracted contours, trying to expand,
tight in one's heart like horses in one's hand.

So that, if something awesome should appear,
something unpromised and unprophesied,
we might dare hope it would not see nor hear,
and might approach, until it came quite near,
deep in itself and self-preoccupied.

ROMAN SARCOPHAGI

Why should we too, though, not anticipate
(set down here and assigned our places thus)
that only for a short time rage and hate
and this bewildering will remain in us,

as in the ornate sarcophagus, enclosed
with images of gods, rings, glasses, trappings,
there lay in slowly self-consuming wrappings
something being slowly decomposed—

till swallowed by those unknown mouths at last,
that never speak. (Where bides a brain that may
yet trust the utterance of its thinking to them?)

Then from the ancient aqueducts there passed
eternal water into them one day—
that mirrors now and moves and sparkles through
    them.

A FEMININE DESTINY

As when, out shooting with his friends, the king
picks up a glass to drink from, any sort—
and afterwards the owner of the thing
preserves it like the rarest ever wrought:

Fate, also thirsty, now and then maybe
has raised a woman to its lips and drunk,
whom then some little life has too much shrunk
from fear of breaking and has carefully

placed in that tremulous vitrine, wherein
its various preciousnesses are consigned
(or objects such as pass for precious there).

As strange as if on loan she's stood therein
and simply gone on growing old and blind
and wasn't precious and was never rare.

GOING BLIND

She'd sat just like the others there at tea.
And then I'd seemed to notice that her cup
was being a little differently picked up.
She'd smiled once. It had almost hurt to see.

And when eventually they rose and talked
and slowly, and as chance led, were dispersing
through several rooms there, laughing and
     conversing,
I noticed her. Behind the rest she walked

subduedly, like someone who presently
will have to sing, and with so many listening;
on those bright eyes of hers, with pleasure glistening,
played, as on pools, an outer radiancy.

She followed slowly and she needed time,
as though some long ascent were not yet by;
and yet: as though, when she had ceased to climb,
she would no longer merely walk, but fly.

DEATH EXPERIENCED

We know just nothing of this going hence
that so excludes us. We've no grounds at all
to greet with plaudits or malevolence
the Death whom that mask-mouth of tragical

lament disfigures so incredibly.
The world's still full of parts being acted by us.
Till pleasing in them cease to occupy us,
Death will act too, although unpleasingly.

When, though, you went, there broke upon this scene
a shining segment of realities
in at the crack you disappeared through: green
of real green, real sunshine, real trees.

We go on acting. Uttering what exacted
such painful learning, gesturing now and then;
but your existence and the part you acted,
withdrawn now from our play and from our ken,

sometimes recur to us like intimations
of that reality and of its laws,
and we transcend awhile our limitations
and act our lives unthinking of applause.

IN THE DRAWING-ROOM

How presently around us they all are,
these noblemen in ruffs and courtier's dress,
each like an evening round his order-star
darkening with ever more remorselessness;
these ladies, slender, fragile, whom their clothes
so much enlarge, with one hand in repose,
small as the collar for a tiny hound:
how they stand round us: round the reader, round
the contemplator of these bibelots,
among which there are some they still possess.

They let us go on, in their tactfulness,
living the kind of life we find alluring
and they can't grasp. They chose florescency,
and flowers are beautiful; we choose maturing,
and that means effort and obscurity.

SELF-PORTRAIT FROM THE YEAR 1906

The old, long-noble race's unregressing
distinction in the eye-brow's archingness.
The gaze with childhood's blue and anxiousness
still in it, far from servile, but confessing
a server's and a woman's humbleness.
The mouth made like a mouth, large, strict, and less
apt for persuading than for just expressing
what's right. The forehead, not unprepossessing,
at home in quiet down-looking shadowedness.

This, as coherence, only just divined;
never, as yet, in suffering or elation
collected for some lasting culmination;
as if from far, though, with stray things, creation
of something real and serious were designed.

THE COURTESAN

The sun of Venice in my hair's preparing
a gold where lustrously shall culminate
all alchemy. My brows, which emulate
her bridges, you can contemplate

over the silent perilousness repairing
of eyes which some communion secretly
unites with her canals, so that the sea
rises and ebbs and changes in them. He

who once has seen me falls to envying
my dog, because, in moments of distraction,
this hand no fieriness incinerates,

scathless, bejewelled, there recuperates.—
And many a hopeful youth of high extraction
will not survive my mouth's envenoming.

THE STEPS OF THE ORANGERY
Versailles

Like kings who simply pace at certain hours
with no more purpose than the habitude
of showing the double-rank of courtly bowers
their presence in their mantle's solitude—

even so this flight of steps ascends in lonely
pomp between pillars bowing eternally:
slowly and By the Grace of God and only
to Heaven and nowhere intermediately;

as having ordered all its retinue
to stay behind—and they're not even daring
to follow at a distance; none may do
so much as hold the heavy train it's wearing.

ROMAN FOUNTAIN

Borghese

Two basins, this one over that, ascending
from an old marbled pool's embosoming,
and, from the upper, water gently bending
to water which below stood proffering

that gentle murmurer silence for reply there,
and, as in hollowed hand, clandestinely
showing it a green- and darkness-curtained sky there
like some unrecognized reality;

itself serenely in its lovely chalice
unhomesickly outspreading, ring on ring,
just sometimes dreamily downladdering,

drop after drop, along the mossy tresses
to the last mirror, that would gently bring
its bowl's convex to smile with changefulnesses.

THE MERRY-GO-ROUND

Jardin du Luxembourg

With roof and shadow for a while careers
the stud of horses, variously bright,
all from that land that long remains in sight
before it ultimately disappears.
Several indeed pull carriages, with tight-
held rein, but all have boldness in their bearing;
with them a wicked scarlet lion's faring
and now and then an elephant all white.

Just as in woods, a stag comes into view,
save that it has a saddle and tied fast
thereon a little maiden all in blue.

And on the lion a little boy is going,
whose small hot hands hold on with all his might,
while raging lion's tongue and teeth are showing.

And now and then an elephant all white.

And on the horses the come riding past,
girls too, bright-skirted, whom the horse-jumps here
scarce now preoccupy: in full career
elsewhither, hitherwards, a glance they cast—

And now and then an elephant all white.

And on it goes and hastens to be ended,
and aimlessly rotates until it's done.
A red, a green, a gray is apprehended,
a little profile, scarcely yet begun.—

And now and then a smile, for us intended,
blissfully happy, dazzlingly expended
upon this breathless, blindly followed fun . . .

SPANISH DANCER

As in the hand a sulphur match, sheer white
before it flames, will stretch out scintillating
tongues on all sides, her round dance, in the tight
ring of spectators, hasty, hot, alight,
has started scintillatingly dilating.

And suddenly it's only flame that's there.

With one glance she has set alight her hair,
and all at once with daring artfulness
spins her whole dress into this fieriness,
from which, like serpents terribly abashing,
her naked arms stretch out aroused and gnashing.

And then, as though her fire would not suffice,
she gathers it all up, and in a trice
flings it away with proud gesticulation
and gazes: still in raging conflagration
it's writhing on the ground unyieldingly.—
She, though, inflexible and with a sweet
saluting smile, looks up victoriously
and stamps it out with little steadfast feet.

QUAI DU ROSAIRE

Bruges

The streets are moving with a gentle gait
(like invalids the first time out of door
trying to remember: What was here before?)
and those that come to squares will long await

another street, that, with a single stride,
crosses the water evening's clarified,
wherein, the more things round about are waning,
the mirrored world inhung will be attaining
reality those things have never known.

Did not this city vanish? Now you're shown
it growing (in some unfathomable way)
alert and lucid in transposal there,
as though that life were no such strange affair;
there hang the gardens now with grander air,
there behind windows suddenly aflare
revolves the dance in the estaminets.

Above remained?—Just silence, I opine,
now slowly tasting, with no tasks to ply,
berry on berry from the sweet grape-vine-
cluster of chime that's hanging in the sky.

ORPHEUS. EURYDICE. HERMES.

That was the so unfathomed mine of souls.
And they, like silent veins of silver ore,
were winding through its darkness. Between roots
welled up the blood that flows on to mankind,
like blocks of heavy porphyry in the darkness.
Else there was nothing red.

But here were rocks
and ghostly forests. Bridges over voidness
and that immense, gray, unreflecting pool
that hung above its so far distant bed
like a gray rainy sky above a landscape.
And between meadows, soft and full of patience,
appeared the pale strip of the single pathway,
like a long line of linen laid to bleach.

And on this single pathway they approached.

In front the slender man in the blue mantle,
gazing in dumb impatience straight before him.
His steps devoured the way in mighty chunks
they did not pause to chew; his hands were hanging,
heavy and clenched, out of the falling folds,
no longer conscious of the lightsome lyre,
the lyre which had grown into his left
like twines of rose into a branch of olive.
It seemed as though his senses were divided:
for, while his sight ran like a dog before him,
turned round, came back, and stood, time and again,

distant and waiting, at the path's next turn,
his hearing lagged behind him like a smell.
It seemed to him at times as though it stretched
back to the progress of those other two
who should be following up this whole ascent.
Then once more there was nothing else behind him
but his climb's echo and his mantle's wind.
He, though, assured himself they still were coming;
said it aloud and heard it die away.
They still were coming, only they were two
that trod with fearful lightness. If he durst
but once look back (if only looking back
were not undoing of this whole enterprise
still to be done), he could not fail to see them,
the two light-footers, following him in silence:

The god of faring and distant message,
the traveling-hood over his shining eyes,
the slender wand held out before his body,
the wings around his ankles lightly beating,
and in his left hand, as entrusted, *her.*

She, so belov'd, that from a single lyre
more mourning rose than from all women-
      mourners—
that a whole world of mourning rose, wherein
all things were once more present: wood and vale
and road and hamlet, field and stream and beast—
and that around this world of mourning turned,
even as around the other earth, a sun
and a whole silent heaven full of stars,
a heaven of mourning with disfigured stars—
she, so beloved.

But hand in hand now with that god she walked,
her paces circumscribed by lengthy shroudings,
uncertain, gentle, and without impatience.
Wrapt in herself, like one whose time is near,
she thought not of the man who went before them,
nor of the road ascending into life.
Wrapt in herself she wandered. And her deadness
was filling her like fullness.
Full as a fruit with sweetness and with darkness
was she with her great death, which was so new
that for the time she could take nothing in.

She had attained a new virginity
and was intangible; her sex had closed
like a young flower at the approach of evening,
and her pale hands had grown so disaccustomed
to being a wife, that even the slim god's
endlessly gentle contact as he led her
disturbed her like a too great intimacy.

Even now she was no longer that blond woman
who'd sometimes echoed in the poet's poems,
no longer the broad couch's scent and island,
nor yonder man's possession any longer.

She was already loosened like long hair,
and given far and wide like fallen rain,
and dealt out like a manifold supply.

She was already root.

And when, abruptly,
the god had halted her and, with an anguished
outcry, outspoke the words: He has turned round!—
she took in nothing, and said softly: Who?

But in the distance, dark in the bright exit,
someone or other stood, whose countenance
was indistinguishable. Stood and saw
how, on a strip of pathway between meadows,
with sorrow in his look, the god of message
turned silently to go behind the figure
already going back by that same pathway,
its paces circumscribed by lengthy shroudings,
uncertain, gentle, and without impatience.

THE BOWL OF ROSES

You've seen the flare of anger, seen two boys
bunch themselves up into a ball of something
that was mere hate and roll upon the ground
like a dumb animal attacked by bees;
actors, sky-towering exaggerators,
the crashing downfall of careering horses,
casting away their sight, flashing their teeth
as though the skull were peeling from the mouth.

But now you know how such things are forgotten;
for now before you stands the bowl of roses,

the unforgettable, entirely filled
with that extremity of being and bending,
proffer beyond all power of giving, presence,
that might be ours: that might be our extreme.

Living in silence, endless opening out,
space being used, but without space being taken
from that space which the things around diminish;
absence of outline, like untinted groundwork
and mere Within; so much so strangely tender
and self-illumined—to the very verge—
where do we know of anything like this?

And this: a feeling able to arise
through petals being touched by other petals?
And this: that one should open like an eyelid,
and lying there beneath it simply eyelids,
all of them closed, as though they had to slumber
ten-fold to quench some inward power of vision.
And this, above all: that through all these petals
light has to penetrate. From thousand heavens
they slowly filter out that drop of darkness
within whose fiery glow the mazy bundle
of stamens stirs itself and reaches upwards.

And then the movement in the roses, look:
gestures deflected through such tiny angles,
they'd all remain invisible unless
their rays ran streaming out into the cosmos.

Look at that white one, blissfully unfolded
and standing in the great big open petals
like Venus upright in her mussel shell;
look how that blusher there, as in confusion,
has turned towards a cooler bloom, and how
the cool one is unfeelingly withdrawing;
and how the cold one stands, wrapped in herself,
among those open roses doffing all.
And *what* they doff—the way it can appear
now light, now heavy—like a cloak, a burden,
a wing, a domino—it all depends—
and *how* they doff it: as before the loved one.

What can they *not* be: was that yellow one
that lies there hollow, open, not the rind
upon a fruit, in which that self-same yellow
was the intenser, orange-ruddier juice?
And did her blowing prove too much for this one,
since, touched by air, her nameless rosiness
assumed the bitter after-taste of lilac?
And is not yonder cambric one a dress,
wherein, still soft and breath-warm, clings the vest
flung off along with it among the shadows
of early morning by the woodland pool?
And what's this opalescent porcelain,
so fragile, but a shallow china cup,
and full of little shining butterflies?
And that, containing nothing but herself?

And are not all just that, just self-containing,
if self-containing means: to take the world

and wind and rain and patience of the spring-time
and guilt and restlessness and muffled fate
and somberness of evening earth and even
the melting, fleeing, forming of the clouds
and the vague influence of distant stars,
and change it to a handful of Within?

It now lies heedless in those open roses.

ARCHAIC TORSO OF APOLLO

Though we've not known his unimagined head
and what divinity his eyes were showing,
his torso like a branching street-lamp's glowing,
wherein his gaze, only turned down, can shed

light still. Or else the breast's insurgency
could not be dazzling you, or you discerning
in that slight twist of loins a smile returning
to where was center'd his virility.

Or else this stone would not stand so intact
beneath the shoulders' through-seen cataract
and would not glisten like a wild beast's skin;

and would not keep from all its contours giving
light like a star: for there's no place therein
that does not see you. You must change your living.

LEDA

When first the god set foot there in his need,
the swan's great beauty almost frightened him;
he vanished into it with wits a-swim.
But his deceit onswept him to his deed

before the feelings of that life untried
could be experienced. And, all-robeless, she
knew who that comer in the swan must be,
and knew already that he eyed

what her confused endeavor to withstand
no longer could conceal. The god alighted,
and, necking through the ever-weaker hand,

loosed himself into her he doted on.
Then really felt his plumage and, delighted,
became within her lap entirely swan.

A PROPHET

Such as giant visions have dilated,
scintillating from the fiery train
of the judgments they have contemplated,
gaze his thickly superciliated
eyes, and words are being accumulated
deep within him once again:

not his own (for what could his words settle?
And how temperedly would they be dealt!),
other, harder: chunks of stone and metal,
which, like a volcano, he must melt

till eruptingly he sends them flying
from his mouth whose curses fill the air;
while his forehead like a dog's is trying
conscientiously to bear

what from his the Lord has disengaged:
Him, Him, all would find beyond denial,
if they'd only follow those great dial-
hands that show Him as He is: enraged.

THE TEMPTATION

No, it didn't help him, his inducing
sharp-toothed thorns into his lustful flesh;
all his teeming senses were producing,
with loud screams of labor, fresh

miscreations: leeringly-distorted
faces, partly crawling, partly flying,
nothings, whose maliciousness was eying
him alone, with whom it jointly sported.

Now his senses had proliferated;
for the pack was fruitful in the night,
and with stipple was centuplicated
still more parti-colorfully bright.
And a drink was brewed from their grimacing,
and his hands were grasping cup on cup,
and like thighs the shadow opened up,
warm and as awakened for embracing.—

And he screamed then for the angel, screamed:
And the angel, in his shiningness,
came and hounded all that had outstreamed
back into the saint's own inwardness,

that he might contend there, year by year,
as before, with monstrous generation,
and distill from inner fermentation
God, the still as yet so far from clear.

ADAM

He, on the cathedral's steep ascent,
stands and stares near where the window-rose is,
as if awed by the apotheosis
which, when it had reached its full extent,

set him over these and these below.
And he towers and joys in his duration,
plain-resolved; who started cultivation
first of all mankind, and did not know

how he'd find a way from Eden-garden,
ready-filled with all it could supply,
to the new Earth. God would only harden,

and, instead of granting him his prayer,
kept on threatening he should surely die.
But the man persisted: She will bear.

EVE

She, on the cathedral's vast ascent,
simply stands there near the window-rose,
with the apple in the apple-pose,
ever henceforth guilty-innocent

of the growingness she brought to birth
since that time she lovingly departed
from the old eternities and started
struggling like a young year through the Earth.

Ah, she could have stayed so gladly, though,
just a little longer there, attending
to the sense and concord beasts would show.

But she found the man resolved to go,
so she went out with him, deathwards tending;
and yet God she'd scarcely got to know.

THE BLIND MAN
Paris

Look, his progress interrupts the scene,
absent from his dark perambulation,
like a dark crack's interpenetration
of a bright cup. And, as on a screen,

all reflections things around are making
get depicted on him outwardly.
Just his feeling stirs, as if intaking
little waves of world invisibly:

here a stillness, there a counter-stand—
as if pondering whom to choose, he'll tarry:
then surrenderingly he'll lift his hand,
almost ritually, as if to marry.

THE GROUP
Paris

Like someone gathering a quick posy: so
Chance here is hastily arranging faces,
widens and then contracts their interspaces,
seizes two distant, lets a nearer go,

drops this for that, blows weariness away,
rejects, like weed, a dog from the bouquet,
and pulls headforemost what's too low, as through
a maze of stalks and petals, into view,

and binds it in, quite small, upon the hem;
stretches once more to change and separate,
and just has time, for one last look at them,

to spring back to the middle of the mat
on which, in one split second after that,
the glistening lifter's swelling his own weight.

LATE AUTUMN IN VENICE

The city drifts no longer like a bait now,
upcatching all the days as they emerge.
Brittlier the glassy palaces vibrate now
beneath your gaze. And from each garden verge.

the summer like a bunch of puppets dangles,
headforemost, weary, made away.
Out of the ground, though, from dead forest tangles
volition mounts: as though before next day

the sea-commander must have rigged and ready
the galleys in the sleepless Arsenal,
and earliest morning air be tarred already

by an armada, oaringly outpressing,
and suddenly, with flare of flags, possessing
the great wind, radiant and invincible.

CORRIDA
In Memoriam Montez, 1830

Since, small almost, through the opened door
with upstartled eyes and ears he came
and supposed the baiting picador
and beribboned barbs to be a game,

that wild figure seems now to consist
of an ever-concentrating weight
of accumulated old black hate,
and his head is clenched into a fist,

no more meeting any playfully:
no, but rearing bloody barbs behind
those presented horns, and in his mind
his opponent from eternity,

who, in gold and mauve-pink silk arrayed,
suddenly turns round and, like a swarm
of bees, and as if vexed but undismayed,
lets the baffled beast beneath his arm

rush by—while his burning looks are lifting
up once more in tremulous accord,
as if all that circling throng were drifting
down from their own shine and sombering
and his eyelids' every fluttering,

till, so unexcitedly, unhating,
leaning on himself, deliberating,

into that great wave's refluctuance
over its dispersed precipitance
almost softly he insheathes his sword.

LADY BEFORE THE MIRROR

At the mirror's surface she'll begin
gently melting, like a spice-assortment
in a sleeping draught, her tired deportment;
and she'll let her smiling drop right in.

And she'll wait until the liquidness
rises from it; then she'll pour her hair
in as well, and, lifting out one bare,
marvelous shoulder from her evening-dress,

quietly drink out of her image. Drink,
what a lover would in wild caresses,
tryingly, all mistrust; and never think

of beckoning her maid until she sees
at the mirror's bottom candles, presses,
and a late hour's undissolving lees.

THE FLAMINGOS

Jardin Des Plantes, Paris

In Fragonard-like mirrorings no more
of ail their white and red is proffered to you
than would have been conveyed if one who knew you
had said of her he'd chosen to adore:

"She was still soft with sleep." For if, forsaking
pool for green grass, they stand together there,
rose-stalked, as in some blossoming parterre,
they're taken by themselves with lures more taking

than Phryne's; till they've necked that pallidness
of eye deep into their own downiness,
where black and ripe-fruit-ruddiness are hiding.

A screech of envy rends the aviary;
they, though, in stretched astonishment, are striding,
each singly, into the imaginary.

THE READER

Who knows him, he who's let his face descend
to where a new existency engages,
only the rapid turn of crowded pages
will sometimes violently suspend?

Even his mother could not feel quite sure
it's he, there reading something saturated
with his own shadow. And, clock-regulated,
can we know how much ebbed from him before

he laboringly uplooked: thereby upheaving
all the book's deepness to the light of day,
with eyes which, now outgiving, not receiving,
impinged upon a filled environment:
as quiet children, after lonely play,
will suddenly perceive the situation;
his features, though, in full coordination,
remained forever different.

THE MOUNTAIN

Six-and-thirty and a hundred times
did the painter write the mountain peak,
sundered from it, driven back to seek
(six-and-thirty and a hundred times)

that incomprehensible volcano,
happy, full of trial, expedientless—
while, forever outlined, it would lay no
bridle on its surging gloriousness:

daily in a thousand ways uprearing,
letting each incomparable night
fall away, as being all too tight;
wearing out at once each new appearing,
every shape assumed the shiningmost,
far, opinionless, unsympathizing—
to be suddenly materializing
there behind each crevice like a ghost.

REQUIEM
(1909)

FOR A FRIEND

I have my dead, and I would let them go
and be surprised to see them all so cheerful,
so soon at home in being-dead, so right,
so unlike their repute. You, you alone,
return; brush past me, move about, persist
in knocking something that vibratingly
betrays you. Oh, don't take from me what I
am slowly learning. I'm right; you're mistaken,
if you're disturbed into a home-sick longing
for something here. We transmute it all;
it's not here, we reflect it from ourselves,
from our own being, as soon as we perceive it.

  I thought you'd got much further. It confounds me
that *you* should thus mistake and come, who passed
all other women so in transmutation.
That we were frightened when you died, or, rather,
that your strong death made a dark interruption,
tearing the till-then from the ever-since:
that is our business: to set that in order
will be the work that everything provides us.
But that you too were frightened, even now
are frightened, now, when fright has lost its meaning,
that you are losing some of your eternity,
even a little, to step in here, friend, here,
where nothing yet exists; that in the All,
for the first time distracted and half-hearted,
you did not grasp the infinite ascension
as once you grasped each single thing on earth;
that from the orbit that already held you

the gravitation of some mute unrest
should drag you down to measurable time:
this often wakes me like an entering thief.
If I could say you merely deign to come
from magnanimity, from superabundance,
because you are so sure, so self-possessed,
that you can wander like a child, not frightened
of places where ther're things that happen to one—
but no, you're asking. And that penetrates
right to the bone and rattles like a saw.
Reproach, such as you might bear as a spirit,
bear against me when I withdraw myself
at night into my lungs, into my bowels,
into the last poor chamber of my heart,
such a reproach would not be half so cruel
as this mute asking. What is it you ask?

    Say, shall I travel? Have you left somewhere
a thing behind you, that torments itself
with trying to reach you? Travel to a country
you never saw, although it was as closely
akin to you as one half of your senses?

    I'll voyage on its rivers, set my foot
upon its soil and ask about old customs,
stand talking with the women in their doorways
and pay attention when they call their children.
I will observe how they take on the landscape
outside there in the course of the old labor
of field and meadow; will express a wish
to be presented to the king himself,
and work upon the priests with bribery
to leave me lying before the strongest statue
and then withdraw, shutting the temple doors.

But in conclusion, having learnt so much,
I'll simply watch the animals, that something
of their own way of turning may glide over
into my joints; I'll have a brief existence
within their eyes, that solemnly retain me
and slowly loose me, calmly, without judgment.
I'll make the gardeners repeat by heart
the names of many flowers and so bring back
in pots of lovely proper names a remnant,
a little remnant, of the hundred perfumes.
And I will purchase fruits too, fruits, wherein
that country, sky and all, will re-exist.

For that was what you understood: full fruits.
You used to set them out in bowls before you
and counterpoise their heaviness with colors.
And women too appeared to you as fruits,
and children too, both of them from within
impelled into the forms of their existence.
And finally you saw yourself as fruit,
lifted yourself out of your clothes and carried
that self before the mirror, let it in
up to your gaze; which remained, large, in front,
and did not say: that's me; no, but: this is.
So uninquiring was your gaze at last,
so unpossessive and so truly poor,
it wanted even you no longer: holy.

That's how I would retain you, as you placed
yourself within the mirror, deep within,
and far from all else. Why come differently?
Why thus revoke yourself? Why are you trying
to make me feel that in those amber beads
around your neck there was still something heavy

with such a heaviness as never lurks
in the beyond of tranquil pictures? Why
does something in your bearing bode misfortune?
What makes you read the contours of your body
like lines upon a hand, and me no longer
able to see them but as destiny?

Come to the candle-light. I'm not afraid
to look upon the dead. When they return
they have a right to hospitality
within our gaze, the same as other things.

Come; we'll remain a little while in silence.
Look at this rose, here on my writing-desk:
is not the light around it just as timid
as that round you? It too should not be here.
It ought to have remained or passed away
out in the garden there, unmixed with me—
it stays, unconscious of my consciousness.

Don't be afraid now if I comprehend:
it's rising in me—oh, I must, I must,
even if it kills me, I must comprehend.
Comprehend, that you're here. I comprehend.
Just as a blind man comprehends a thing,
I feel your fate although I cannot name it.
Let both of us lament that someone took you
out of your mirror. If you still can cry?
No, you can't cry. You long ago transformed
the force and thrust of tears to your ripe gazing,
and were in act of changing every kind
of sap within you to a strong existence
that mounts and circles in blind equipoise.

Then, for the last time, chance got hold of you,
and snatched you back out of your farthest progress,
back to a world where saps will have their way.
Did not snatch all, only a piece at first,
but when reality, from day to day,
so swelled around that piece that it grew heavy,
you needed your whole self; then off you went
and broke yourself in fragments from your law,
laboriously, needing yourself. And then
you took yourself away and from your heart's
warm, night-warm, soil you dug the yet green seeds
your death was going to spring from: your own
        death,
the death appropriate to your own life.
And then you ate those grains of your own death
like any others, ate them one by one,
and had within yourself an after-taste
of unexpected sweetness, had sweet lips,
you: in your senses sweet within already.

   Let us lament. Do you know how unwilling
and hesitatingly your blood returned,
recalled from an incomparable orbit?
With what confusion it took up again
the tiny circulation of the body?
With what mistrust it entered the placenta,
suddenly tired from the long homeward journey?
You drove it on again, you pushed it forward,
you dragged it to the hearth, as people drag
a herd of animals to sacrifice;
and spite of all desired it to be happy.
And finally you forced it: it was happy,

and ran up and surrendered. You supposed,
being so accustomed to the other measures,
that this was only for a little while;
but now you were in time, and time is long.
And time goes by, and time goes on, and time
is like relapsing after some long illness.

How very short your life, when you compare it
with hours you used to sit in silence, bending
the boundless forces of your boundless future
out of their course to the new germination,
that became fate once more. O painful labor.
Labor beyond all strength. And you performed it
day after day, you dragged yourself along to it
and pulled the lovely woof out of the loom
and wove your threads into another pattern.
And still had spirit for a festival.

For when you'd done you looked for some reward,
like children, when they've drunk a nasty drink
of bitter-sweet tea that may make one better.
You gave your own reward, being still so distant,
even then, from all the rest; and no one there
who could have hit on a reward to please you.
You yourself knew it. You sat up in child-bed,
a mirror there before you, that returned
all that you gave. Now everything was you,
and right in front; within was mere deceit,
the sweet deceit of Everywoman, gladly
putting her jewels on and doing her hair.

And so you died like women long ago,
died in the old warm house, old-fashionedly,
the death of those in child-bed, who are trying
to close themselves again but cannot do it,

72

because that darkness which they also bore
returns and grows importunate and enters.

Ought they not, though, to have gone and
    hunted up
some mourners for you? Women who will weep
for money, and, if paid sufficiently,
will howl through a whole night when all is still.
Observances! We haven't got enough
observances. All vanishes in talk.
That's why you have to come back, and with me
retrieve omitted mourning. Can you hear me?
I'd like to fling my voice out like a cloth
over the broken fragments of your death
and tug at it till it was all in tatters,
and everything I said was forced to go
clad in the rags of that torn voice and freeze—
if mourning were enough. But I accuse:
not him who thus withdrew you from yourself
(I can't distinguish him, he's like them all),
but in him I accuse all: accuse man.
    If somewhere deep within me rises up
a having-once-been-child I don't yet know,
perhaps the purest childness of my childhood:
I will not know it. Without looking at it
or asking, I will make an angel of it,
and hurl that angel to the foremost rank
of crying angels that remembrance God.
    For now too long this suffering has lasted,
and none can stand it; it's too hard for us,
this tortuous suffering caused by spurious love,

which, building on prescription like a habit,
calls itself just and battens on injustice.
Where is the man who justly may possess?
Who can possess what cannot hold itself
but only now and then blissfully catches
and flings itself on like a child a ball?
As little as the admiral can retain
the Nikê poised upon his vessel's prow
when the mysterious lightness of her godhead
has caught her up into the limpid sea-wind,
can one of us call back to him the woman
who, seeing us no longer, takes her way
along some narrow strip of her existence,
as through a miracle, without mischance—
unless his calling and delight were guilt.

For this is guilt, if anything be guilt,
not to enlarge the freedom of a love
with all the freedom in one's own possession.
All we can offer where we love is this:
to loose each other; for to hold each other
comes easy to us and requires no learning.

Are you still there? Still hiding in some corner?—
You knew so much of all that I've been saying,
and could so much too, for you passed through life
open to all things, like a breaking day.
Women suffer: loving means being lonely,
and artists feel at times within their work
the need, where most they love, for transmutation.
You began both; and both exist in *that*
which fame, detaching it from you, disfigures.

Oh, you were far beyond all fame. Were in-
conspicuous; had gently taken in
your beauty as a gala flag's intaken
on the gray morning of a working-day,
and wanted nothing but a lengthy work—
which is not done; in spite of all, not done.

If you're still there, if somewhere in this darkness
there's still a spot where your perceptive spirit's
vibrating on the shallow waves of sound
a lonely voice within a lonely night
starts in the air-stream of a lofty room:
hear me and help me. Look, without knowing when,
we keep on slipping backwards from our progress
into some unintended thing, and there
we get ourselves involved as in a dream,
and there at last we die without awakening.
No one's got further. Anyone who's lifted
the level of his blood to some long work
may find he's holding it aloft no longer
and that it's worthlessly obeying its weight.
For somewhere there's an old hostility
between our human life and greatest work.
May I see into it and it say: help me!

Do not return. If you can bear it, stay
dead with the dead. The dead are occupied.
But help me, as you may without distraction,
as the most distant sometimes helps: in me.

DUINO ELEGIES
(1923)

THE FIRST ELEGY

Who, if I cried, would hear me among the angelic
orders? And even if one of them suddenly
pressed me against his heart, I should fade
        in the strength of his
stronger existence. For Beauty's nothing
but beginning of Terror we're still just able to bear,
and why we adore it so is because it serenely
disdains to destroy us. Every angel is terrible.
And so I repress myself, and swallow the call-note
of depth-dark sobbing. Alas, who is there
we can make use of? Not angels, not men;
and even the noticing beasts are aware
that we don't feel very securely at home
in this interpreted world. There remains, perhaps,
some tree on a slope, to be looked at day after day,
there remains for us yesterday's walk and
        the long-drawn loyalty
of a habit that liked us and stayed and never
        gave notice.
Oh, and there's Night, there's Night, when wind full
        of cosmic space
feeds on our faces: for whom would she not remain,
longed for, mild disenchantress, painfully there
for the lonely heart to achieve? Is she lighter
        for lovers?
Alas, with each other they only conceal their lot!
Don't you know *yet*?—Fling the emptiness out of
        your arms
to broaden the spaces we breathe—maybe that
        the birds
will feel the extended air in more fervent flight.

Yes, the Springs had need of you. Many a star
was waiting for you to perceive it. Many a wave
would rise in the past towards you; or else, perhaps,
as you went by an open window, a violin
would be utterly giving itself. All this was
      commission.
But were you equal to it? Were you not still
distraught by expectancy, as though all were
      announcing
some beloved's approach? (As if you could hope
to house her, with all those great strange thoughts
going in and out and often staying overnight!)
Should you be longing, though, sing the great lovers:
      the fame
of all they can feel is far from immortal enough.
Those—you envied them almost, those forsaken,
      you found
so far beyond the requited in loving. Begin
ever anew their never-attainable praise.
Consider: the Hero continues, even his setting
was a pretext for further existence, an ultimate birth.
But lovers are taken back by exhausted Nature
into herself, as though such creative force
could not be exerted twice. Does Gaspara Stampa
mean enough to you yet, and that any girl, whose
      beloved
has slipped away, might feel, from that far intenser
example of loving: "Could I but become like her!"?
Should not these oldest sufferings be finally growing
fruitfuller for us? Is it not time that, in loving,
we freed ourselves from the loved one, and,
      quivering, endured:

as the arrow endures the string, to become, in
        the gathering out-leap,
something more than itself? For staying is nowhere.

Voices, voices. Hearken, my heart, as only
saints once hearkened: so, that the giant call
lifted them off the ground; they, though, impossibles,
went on kneeling and paid no heed:
such was their hearkening. Not that you could
        bear God's
voice, by a long way. But hark to the suspiration,
the uninterrupted news that grows out of silence.
Rustling towards you now from those youthfully-
        dead.
Whenever you entered a church in Rome or in Naples
were you not always being quietly addressed by
        their fate?
Or else an inscription sublimely imposed itself on
        you,
as, lately, the tablet in Santa Maria Formosa.
What they require of me? that I should gently remove
the appearance of suffered injustice, that hinders
a little, at times, their purely-proceeding spirits.

True, it is strange to inhabit the earth no longer,
to use no longer customs scarcely acquired,
not to interpret roses, and other things
that promise so much, in terms of a human future;
to be no longer all that one used to be
in endlessly anxious hands, and to lay aside
even one's proper name like a broken toy.

Strange, not to go on wishing one's wishes. Strange,
to see all that was once relation so loosely fluttering
hither and thither in space. And it's hard, being dead,
and full of retrieving before one begins to perceive
a little eternity.—All of the living, though,
make the mistake of drawing too sharp distinctions.
Angels (it's said) would be often unable to tell
whether they moved among living or dead.
     The eternal
torrent whirls all the ages through either realm
for ever, and sounds above their voices in both.

They've finally no more need of us, the early-
     departed,
one's gently weaned from terrestrial things as
     one mildly
outgrows the breasts of a mother. But we, that have
     need of
such mighty secrets, we, for whom sorrow's so often
source of blessedest progress, could we exist
     without them?
Is the story in vain, how once, in the mourning
     for Linos,
venturing earliest music pierced barren numbness,
     and how,
in the startled space an almost deified youth
suddenly quitted for ever, emptiness first
felt the vibration that now lifts us and comforts
     and helps?

THE FOURTH ELEGY

O trees of life, what are your signs of winter?
We're not at one. We've no instinctive knowledge,
like migratory birds. Outstript and late,
we force ourselves on winds and find no welcome
from ponds where we alight. We comprehend
flowering and fading simultaneously.
And somewhere lions still roam, all unaware,
while yet their splendor lasts, of any weakness.

We, though, while we're intent upon one thing,
can feel the cost and conquest of another.
The Next's our enemy. Aren't lovers always
coming to precipices in each other—
lovers, that looked for spaces, hunting, home?
Then, for the sudden sketchwork of a moment,
a ground of contrast's painfully prepared,
to make us see it. For they're very clear
with us, we that don't know our feeling's shape,
but only that which forms it from outside.
Who's not sat tense before his own heart's curtain?
Up it would go: the scenery was Parting.
Easy to understand. The well-known garden,
swaying a little. Then appeared the dancer.
Not *him*! Enough! However light he foots it,
he's just disguised, and turns into a bourgeois,
and passes through the kitchen to his dwelling.
I will not have these half-filled masks! No, no,
rather the doll. That's full. I'll force myself
to bear the husk, the wire, and even that face
of sheer appearance. Here! I'm in my seat.

Even if the lights go out, even if I'm told
"There's nothing more"—even if grayish drafts
of emptiness come drifting from the stage—
even if of all my silent forbears none
sits by me any longer, not a woman,
not even the boy with the brown squinting eyes:
I'll still remain. For one can always watch.

Am I not right? You, to whom life would taste
so bitter, Father, when you tasted mine,
that turbid first infusion of my Must,
you kept on tasting as I kept on growing,
and, still arrested by the after-taste
of such queer future, tried my clouded gaze—
you, who so often, since you died, my Father,
have been afraid within my inmost hope,
surrendering realms of that serenity
the dead are lords of for my bit of fate—
am I not right? And you, am I not right—
you that would love me for that small beginning
of love for you I always turned away from,
because the space within your faces changed,
even while I loved it, into cosmic space
where you no longer were . . . when I feel like it,
to wait before the puppet stage—no, rather
gaze so intensely on it that at last
a counterpoising angel has to come
and play a part there, snatching up the husks?
Angel and doll! Then there's at last a play.
Then there unites what we continually
part by our mere existence. Then at last

emerges from our seasons here the cycle
of the whole process. Over and above us,
then, there's the angel playing. Look, the dying—
surely they must suspect how full of pretext
is all that we accomplish here, where nothing
is what it really is. O hours of childhood,
hours when behind the figures there was more
than the mere past, and when what lay before us
was not the future! True, we were growing,
      and sometimes
made haste to be grown up, half for the sake
of those who'd nothing left but their grown-upness.
Yet, when alone, we entertained ourselves
with everlastingness: there we would stand,
within the gap left between world and toy,
upon a spot which, from the first beginning,
had been established for a pure event.

Who'll show a child just as it is? Who'll place it
within its constellation, with the measure
of distance in its hand? Who'll make its death
from gray bread, that grows hard—or leave it there,
within the round mouth, like the seeded core
of a nice apple? . . . . . . Minds of murderers
can easily be fathomed. This, though: death,
the whole of death, before life's start, to hold it
so gently and so free from all resentment,
transcends description.

THE EIGHTH ELEGY

Dedicated to Rudolf Kassner

With all its eyes the creature-world beholds
the open. But our eyes, as though reversed,
encircle it on every side, like traps
set round its unobstructed path to freedom.
What *is* outside, we know from the brute's face
alone; for while a child's quite small we take it
and turn it round and force it to look backwards
at conformation, not that openness
so deep within the brute's face. Free from death.
We alone see *that*; the free animal
has its decease perpetually behind it
and God in front, and when it moves, it moves
within eternity, like running springs.
We've never, no, not for a single day,
pure space before us, such as that which flowers
endlessly open into: always world,
and never nowhere without no: that pure,
unsuperintended element one breathes,
endlessly knows, and never craves. A child
sometimes gets quietly lost there, to be always
jogged back again. Or someone dies and *is* it.
For, nearing death, one perceives death no longer,
and stares ahead—perhaps with large brute gaze.
Lovers—were not the other present, always
blocking the view!—draw near to it and wonder . . .
Behind the other, as though through oversight,
the thing's revealed . . . But no one gets beyond
the other, and so world returns once more.

Always facing Creation, we perceive there
only a mirroring of the free and open,
dimmed by our breath. Or that a dumb brute's
        calmly
raising its head to look us through and through.
For this is Destiny: being opposite,
and nothing else, and always opposite.

Did consciousness such as we have exist
in the sure animal that moves towards us
upon a different course, the brute would drag us
round in its wake. But its own being for it
is infinite, inapprehensible,
unintrospective, pure, like its outgazing.
Where we see Future, it sees Everything,
itself in Everything, for ever healed.

And yet, within the wakefully-warm beast
there lies the weight and care of a great sadness.
For that which often overwhelms us clings
to him as well—a kind of memory
that what one's pressing after now was once
nearer and truer and attached to us
with infinite tenderness. Here all is distance,
there it was breath. Compared with that first home
the second seems ambiguous and fickle.

Oh, bliss of *tiny* creatures that *remain*
for ever in the womb that brought them forth!
Joy of the gnat, that can still leap *within,*
even on its wedding-day: for womb is all!

Look at the half-assurance of the bird,
through origin almost aware of both,
like one of those Etruscan souls, escaped
from a dead man enclosed within a space
on which his resting figure forms a lid.
And how dismayed is any womb-born thing
that has to fly! As though it were afraid
of its own self, it zigzags through the air
like crack through cup. The way a bat's track runs
rendingly through the evening's porcelain.

And we, spectators always, everywhere,
looking at, never out of, everything!
It fills us. We arrange it. It collapses.
We re-arrange it, and collapse ourselves.

Who's turned us round like this, so that we always,
do what we may, retain the attitude
of someone who's departing? Just as he,
on the last hill, that shows him all his valley
for the last time, will turn and stop and linger,
we live our lives, for ever taking leave.

THE NINTH ELEGY

Why, when this span of life might be fleeted away
as laurel, a little darker than all
the surrounding green, with tiny waves on the border

of every leaf (like the smile of a wind)—oh, why
have to be human, and, shunning Destiny,
long for Destiny? . . .

                              Not because happiness really
exists, that precipitate profit of imminent loss.
Not out of curiosity, not just to practice the heart,
that could still be there in laurel. . . . . .
But because being here is much, and because all this
that's here, so fleeting, seems to require us
        and strangely
concerns us. Us the most fleeting of all. Just once,
everything, only for once. Once and no more.
        And we, too,
once. And never again. But this
having been once, though only once,
having been once on earth—can it ever be cancelled?

And so we keep pressing on and trying to perform it,
trying to contain it within our simple hands,
in the more and more crowded gaze, in
        the speechless heart.
Trying to become it. To give it to whom? We'd rather
hold on to it all for ever . . . But into the other relation,
what, alas! do we carry across? Not the beholding
        we've here
slowly acquired, and no here occurrence. Not one.
Sufferings, then. Above all, the hardness of life,
the long experience of love; in fact,
purely untellable things. But later,
under the stars, what use? the more deeply
        untellable stars?

Yet the wanderer too doesn't bring from mountain
    to valley
a handful of earth, of for all untellable earth, but only
a word he has won, pure, the yellow and blue
gentian. Are we, perhaps, *here* just for saying:
    House,
Bridge, Fountain, Gate, Jug, Fruit tree, Window,—
possibly: Pillar, Tower? . . . but for *saying,*
    remember,
oh, for such saying as never the things themselves
hoped so intensely to be. Is not the secret purpose
of this sly Earth, in urging a pair of lovers,
just to make everything leap with ecstasy in them?
Threshold: what does it mean
to a pair of lovers, that they should be wearing
    their own
worn threshold a little, they too, after the many
    before,
before the many to come . . . as a matter of course!

  Here is the time for the Tellable, *here* is its home.
Speak and proclaim. More than ever
things we can live with are falling away, for that
which is oustingly taking their place is an
    imageless act.
Act under crusts, that will readily split as soon
as the doing within outgrows them and takes
    a new outline.
Between the hammers lives on
our heart, as between the teeth
the tongue, which, in spite of all,
still continues to praise.

Praise this world to the Angel, not the untellable: you
can't impress him with the splendor you've felt; in
    the cosmos
where he more feelingly feels you're only a novice. So
    show him
some simple thing, refashioned by age after age,
till it lives in our hands and eyes as a part of
    ourselves.
Tell him *things*. He'll stand more astonished: as
    you did
beside the roper in Rome or the potter in Egypt.
Show him how happy a thing can be, how guileless
    and ours;
how even the moaning of grief purely determines
    on form,
serves as a thing, or dies into a thing—to escape
to a bliss beyond the fiddle. These things that live
    on departure
understand when you praise them: fleeting, they
    look for
rescue through something in us, the most fleeting of
    all.
Want us to change them entirely, within our
    invisible hearts,
into—oh, endlessly—into ourselves! Whosoever we
    are.

Earth, is it not just this that you want: to arise
invisibly in us? Is not your dream
to be one day invisible? Earth! invisible!
What is your urgent command, if not transformation?

Earth, you darling, I will! Oh, believe me, you need
no more of your spring-times to win me over:
    a single one,
ah, one, is already more than my blood can endure.
Beyond all names I am yours, and have been for ages.
You were always right, and your holiest inspiration
is Death, that friendly Death.
Look, I am living. On what? Neither childhood
    nor future
are growing less. . . . . Supernumerous existence
wells up in my heart.

SONNETS TO ORPHEUS
(1923)

.

A GOD CAN DO IT

A god can do it. But can a man expect
to penetrate the narrow lyre and follow?
His sense is discord. Temples for Apollo
are not found where two heart-ways intersect.

For song, as taught by you, is not desire,
not wooing of something finally attained;
song is existence. For the god unstrained.
But when shall we *exist*? And he require

the earth and heavens to exist for us?
It's more than being in love, boy, though
        your ringing
voice may have flung your dumb mouth open thus:

learn to forget those fleeting ecstasies.
Far other is the breath of real singing.
An aimless breath. A stirring in the God. A breeze.

RAISE NO COMMEMORATING STONE

Raise no commemorating stone. The roses
shall blossom every summer for his sake.
For this is Orpheus. His metamorphosis
in this one and in that. We should not make

searches for other names. Once and for all,
it's Orpheus when there's song. He comes and goes.
Is it not much if sometimes, by some small
number of days, he shall outlive the rose?

Could you but feel his passing's needfulness!
Though he himself may dread the hour
        drawing nigher
Already, when his words pass earthliness,

he passes with them far beyond your gaze.
His hands unhindered by the trellised lyre,
in all his over-steppings he obeys.

PRAISING, THAT'S IT!

Praising, that's it! As a praiser and blesser
he came like the ore from the taciturn mine.
Came with his heart, oh, transient presser,
for men, of a never-exhaustible wine.

Voice never fails him for things lacking luster,
sacred example will open his mouth.
All becomes vineyard, all becomes cluster,
warmed by his sympathy's ripening south.

Crypts and the moldering kings who lie there
do not belie his praising, neither
doubt, when a shadow obscures our days.

He is a messenger always attendant,
reaching far through their gates resplendent
dishes of fruit for the dead to praise.

MIRRORS

Mirrors: no one has yet distilled with
patient knowledge your fugitive
essence. You spaces in time, that are filled with
holes like those of a sieve.

Squandering the empty ball-room's pomp,
deep as forests when twilight broods . . .
And, like sixteen-pointers, the lusters romp
through your virginal solitudes.

Pictures crowd you at times. A few
seem to be taken right within you,
shyly to others you wave adieu.

There, though, the fairest will always be,
till through to her lips withheld continue
Narcissus, released into lucency.

THIS IS THE CREATURE

This is the creature there has never been.
They never knew it, and yet, none the less,
they loved the way it moved, its suppleness,
its neck, its very gaze, mild and serene.

Not there, because they loved it, it behaved
as though it were. They always left some space.
And in that clear unpeopled space they saved
it lightly reared its head, with scarce a trace

of not being there. They fed it, not with corn,
but only with the possibility
of being. And that was able to confer

such strength, its brow put forth a horn. One horn
Whitely it stole up to a maid—to *be*
within the silver mirror and in her.

O FOUNTAIN MOUTH

O fountain mouth, you mouth that can respond
so inexhaustibly to all who ask
with one, pure, single saying. Marble mask
before the water's flowing face. Beyond,

the aqueducts' long derivation. Past
the tombs, from where the Apennines begin,
they bring your saying to you, which at last,
over the grizzled age of your dark chin,

falls to the waiting basin, crystal-clear;
falls to the slumbering recumbent ear,
the marble ear, with which you will confer.

One of earth's ears. With her own lonely mood
she thus converses. Let a jug intrude,
she'll only think you've interrupted her.

STILL THE GOD REMAINS

Still the god remains an ever-growing
wholeness we have irritably burst.
We are sharp, for we insist on knowing,
he exists serenely and dispersed.

Even gifts of purest consecration
only find acceptance in so much
as he turns in moveless contemplation
to the end we do not touch.

Only those who dwell
out of sight can taste the spring we hear,
when the god has silently assented.

With its brawling we must be contented.
And the lamb's more silent instinct's clear
when it begs us for its bell.

DANCER

Dancer: you transmutation
of all going-by into going: what you have wrought!
And your finishing whirl, that tree of mere
        animation,
how it took over the year you had flyingly caught!

Did not its crown, that your swaying might settle
        to swarming,
suddenly blossom with stillness? Above that, too,
was there not sunnily, was there not summerly
        warming
all the warmth that exhaled from you?

Nay, it was able, your tree of rapture, to bear.
Are they not, all its fruits that so peacefully shine,
jug streaked with ripeness, vase further ripened,
        still there?

And does not your mark in their paintings still meet
        the discerning—
that of your eyebrows' darker line
swiftly inscribed on the wall of your own swift
        turning?

HOW IT THRILLS US

How it thrills us, the bird's clear cry . . .
Any cry that was always there.
Children, playing in the open air,
children already go crying by

real cries. Cry chance in. Through crevasses
in that same space whereinto, as dreaming
men into dreams, the pure bird-cry passes
they drive their splintering wedge of screaming.

Where are we? Freer and freer, we gyre
only half up, kites breaking
loose, with our frills of laughter flaking

away in the wind.—Make the criers a choir,
singing god! that resurgently waking
may bear on its waters the head and the lyre.

DOES IT EXIST?

Does it exist, though, Time the destroyer?
When will it scatter the tower on the resting hill?
This heart, the eternal gods' eternal enjoyer,
when shall the Demiurge ravish and spill?

Are we really such tremblingly breakable
things as Destiny tries to pretend?
Does childhood's promise, deep, unmistakable,
down in the roots, then, later, end?

Ah, Mutability's specter!
out through the simple accepter
you, like a vapor, recede.

We, though we wax but for waning,
fill none the less for remaining
powers a celestial need.

POEMS 1906–26

TURNING

The way from intensity to greatness leads through sacrifice.—Kassner

Long he'd outwrung it with gazing.
Stars collapsed on their knees
under that wrestlerish uplook.
Or he would kneelingly gaze
and his instancy's perfume
tired an immortal until
it smiled at him out of its sleep.

He gazed at towers so hard,
he filled them with terror:
building them up again, suddenly, all in a moment.
And yet how often the day-
over-laden landscape
sank to rest in his calm perception at evening!

Animals trustfully entered
his open glance as they pastured,
and the imprisoned lions
stared as into incomprehensible freedom.
Birds flew straight through him,
kindly soul. Flowers
gazed back into him
large as to children.

And report that a *seer* was there
stirred those less,
more doubtfully, visible
creatures, women.

Gazing, since when?
How long fervently fasting,
with glance that at bottom besought?

When, waiting, he lived in foreign lands; the inn's
distracted, alienated room
morosely around him; within the avoided mirror
once more the room,
and then, from his harrowing bed,
the room again—
airy councils were held,
inapprehensible councils,
about his still, through the painfully cumbered body,
still preceptible heart:
councils unoverheard
judged that it had not love.

(Further consecrations withheld.)

For gazing, look, has a limit.
And the on-gazeder world
wants to mature in love.

Work of sight is achieved,
now for some heart-work
on all those images, prisoned within you; for you
overcame them, but do not know them as yet.
Behold, O man within, the maiden within you!—
creature wrung from a thousand natures, creature
only outwrung, but never,
as yet, belov'd.

HYMN

August 1914

For the first time I see you rising,
hearsaid, remote, incredible War God.
How thickly our peaceful corn was intersown
with terrible action, suddenly grown mature!
Small even yesterday, needing nurture, and now
tall as a man: tomorrow
towering beyond man's reach. Before we know it,
    he's there,
the glowing god himself, tearing his crop
out of the nation's roots, and harvest begins.
Up whirl the human sheaves to the human
    thunder-storm. Summer
is left behind among the sports on the green.
Playing children remain there, remembering elders,
trustful women. The universal parting
mingles with moving fragrance of blossoming limes,
whose heavy scent will hold a meaning for years.
Brides are more chosenly walking, as though not only
one life had united with theirs, but a whole people
set their affections in tune. With slowly
    measuring gaze
boys encircle the youth that already belongs
to the more adventurous future: he, who has
    stood perplexed
in the web of a hundred contradictory voices—
oh, how the single call has lightened his life!
    For what,
beside this, the one thing needful, would not seem
    merest caprice?

A god at last! Since the God of Peace so often
eluded our grasp, the God of Battles has grasped us,
hurling his bolt: while over the heart full of home
screams his thunderous dwelling, his scarlet heaven.

EVERYTHING BECKONS TO US

Everything beckons to us to perceive it,
murmurs at every turn 'Remember me!'
A day we passed, too busy to receive it,
will yet unlock us all its treasury.

Who shall compute our harvest? Who shall bar
us from the former years, the long-departed?
What have we learnt from living since we started,
except to find in others what we are?

Except to re-enkindle commonplace?
O house, O sloping field, O setting sun!
Your features form into a face, you run,
you cling to us, returning our embrace!

One space spreads through all creatures equally—
inner-world-space. Birds quietly flying go
flying through us. Oh, I that want to grow,
the tree I look outside at grows in me!

It stands in me, that house I look for still,
in me that shelter I have not possessed.
I, the now well-beloved: on my breast
this fair world's image clings and weeps her fill.

EXPOSED ON THE HEART'S MOUNTAINS

Exposed on the heart's mountains. Look, how
        small there!
look, the last hamlet of words, and, higher,
(but still how small!) yet one remaining
farmstead of feeling: d'you see it?
Exposed on the heart's mountains. Virgin rock
under the hands. Though even here
something blooms: from the dumb precipice
an unknowing plant blooms singing into the air.
But what of the knower? Ah, he began to know
and holds his peace, exposed on the heart's
        mountains.
While, with undivided mind,
many, maybe, many well-assured mountain beasts,
pass there and pause. And the mighty sheltered bird
circles the summits' pure refusal.—But, oh,
no longer sheltered, here on the heart's mountains . . .

TO MUSIC

The Property of Frau Hanna Wolff

Music: breathing of statues. Perhaps:
stillness of pictures. You speech, where speeches
end. You time,
vertically posed on the courses of vanishing hearts.

Feelings for what? Oh, you transformation
of feelings into . . . audible landscape!
You stranger: Music. Space that's outgrown us,
heart-space. Innermost us, transcendently
surging away from us—holiest parting,
where what is within surrounds us
as practised horizon, as other
side of the air,
pure,
gigantic,
no longer lived in.

WHEN WILL, WHEN WILL

Given to M.

. . . When will, when will, when will it have reached
    saturation,
this praising and lamentation? Has not all incantation
in human words been decanted by master-magicians?
    O vanity
of further experimentation! Is not humanity
battered by books as though by continual bells?

Perceiving, between two books, the silent heaven,
      or else
a segment of simple earth in evening light, rejoice!

Louder than storms, than oceans, the human voice
has cried . . . What infinite overbalance of stillness
there must be in cosmic space, since the
      grasshopper's shrillness
stayed audible over our cries, and the stars appear
silently there in the ether above our shrieking!

Would that our farthest, old and oldest fathers
      were speaking!
And we: hearers at last! The first of all men to hear.

THE MAGICIAN

He calls it up. It shrinks together. Stays.
What stays? The Other; everything outside him
becomes a creature. And the thing displays
a swiftly made-up face that can deride him.

Prevail, magician, oh, prevail, prevail!
Create an equipoise. Cause no vibration:
you and the house have got to hold the scale
against the weight of all that augmentation.

Decision falls. The spell begins anew.
He knows, the call has countered the denial.
His face, though, stands at midnight, like a dial
with hands coincident. He's spell-bound too.

FOR WITOLD HULEWICZ

Happy who know that behind all speeches
still the unspeakable lies;
that it's from there that greatness reaches
us in the form we prize!

Trusting not to the diversely fashioned
bridges of difference we outfling:
so that we gaze out of every impassioned
joy at some wholly communal thing.

EROS

Masks! Masks! Or blind him! How can they endure
this flaming Eros gods and men obey,
bursting in summer-solstice on the pure
idyllic prologue to their vernal play?

How imperceptibly the conversation
takes a new, graver turn . . . A cry . . . And, there!

he's flung the nameless fascination
like a dim temple round the fated pair.

Lost, lost! O instantaneous perdition!
In brief divinity they cling.
Life turns, and Destiny begins her mission.
And within there weeps a spring.

THE SAP IS MOUNTING BACK

The sap is mounting back from that unseenness
darkly renewing in the common deep,
back to the light, and feeding the pure greenness
hiding in rinds round which the winds still weep.

The inner side of Nature is reviving.
another *sursum corda* will resound;
invisibly, a whole year's youth is striving
to climb those trees that look so iron-bound.

Preserving still that grey and cool expression,
the ancient walnut's filling with event;
while the young brush-wood trembles with
        repression
under the perching bird's presentiment.

113

WORLD WAS IN THE FACE OF THE BELOVED

World was in the face of the beloved—
but was poured out all of a sudden:
world is outside, can't be comprehended.

Why did I not drink, then, when I raised it,
drink from the full face of the beloved,
world—so near, I tasted its bouquet?

Oh, I did! I drank insatiably.
Only, I was so brim-full already
with world, that when I drank I overflowed.

THE GOLDSMITH

Coaxing chain-links, castigating rings,
"Wait! Go slowly!" is my constant cry:
"Outside there'll be happenings by and by."
Things, I keep repeating, Things, Things, Things,
as I ply my smith-craft: for till I
reach them, none can set up on its own
or undertake the tiniest career.
All, by grace of God, are equal here:
I, the gold, the fire, and the stone.

"Gently, ruby, drop that raging tone!
This pale pearl is trembling, and the flowing
tears have started in the beryl-stone.
Now you've rested, it's sheer terror, going
round among you, as you leap from sleep."
Bluely coruscating, redly glowing,
how they sparkle at me from the heap!

Gold, though, seems to know what I require,
for I've tamed its spirit in the fire;
still, I have to coax it carefully
round the gem; and suddenly, in grasping
that, the savage creature thrusts its rasping
claws with metal hatred into me.

R. M. R.
4 December 1875–29 December 1926

ROSE, OH THE PURE CONTRADICTION,
DELIGHT, OF BEING NO ONE'S SLEEP UNDER
SO MANY LIDS.

NOTES

NEW POEMS

DAVID SINGS BEFORE SAUL
I Samuel, xvi, 14–23.

THE DEPARTURE OF THE PRODIGAL SON
Luke, xv, 11–32.

THE OLIVE GARDEN
Luke, xxii, 39–46.

THE POET'S DEATH
Probably suggested by Rodin's sculpture, *La Morte du Poète.*

BUDDHA
On a little mound in Rodin's garden at Meudon stood an image of Buddha, which Rilke could see from his window and to which he often refers in his letters.

THE CATHEDRAL
and in those towers: Rilke had been struck by the contrast between the spireless towers of so many medieval French cathedrals (Chartres, Notre-Dame, Rheims, Amiens, etc.) and the spired towers of most German and Austrian ones.

THE GAZELLE
Rilke had written to his wife in June 1907 (a month before this poem was written): "Yesterday, by the way, I spent the whole morning in the Jardin des Plantes, in front of the

gazelles . . . I saw only one of them stand up for a moment, it lay down again immediately; but I saw, while they were stretching and testing themselves, the magnificent workmanship of those limbs: (they are like guns, from which leaps are fired)."

DEATH EXPERIENCED
In memory of Countess Louise Schwerin, who had died 24 January 1906.

IN THE DRAWING-ROOM
Inspired by a visit to Chantilly.

THE MERRY-GO-ROUND
all from that land: "that land" is Childhood, and the image of that of a coastline gradually sinking beneath the horizon from the gaze of a departing voyager.

ADAM and EVE
The two figures by Viollet-le-Duc on the facade of Notre-Dame.

CORRIDA
It was in 1830, as Rilke informed his wife in a letter (6 September 1907) enclosing this and another poem, that the torero Francisco Montez first practiced what afterwards became an established technique, namely, to step aside from the path of the charging bull and to dispatch the baffled animal when it returned. A portrait of Montez, "in gold and mauve-pink silk," by Eugenio Lucas the elder (1824–70) was for many years on loan at the Kaiser Friederich Museum in Berlin, which Rilke often visited. At the time when he wrote this poem he had never been in Spain or seen a bull-fight (*corrida*).

THE MOUNTAIN
Hokusai and his numerous paintings ("writings") of the volcano Fujiyama.

117

REQUIEM

FOR A FRIEND

The friend was Paula Modersohn-Becker (1876–1907), perhaps
the only painter of real genius among those whom Rilke met
while staying in the artists' colony of Worpswede in 1900.
Shortly after his own marriage to her friend Clara Westhoff in
April 1901, Paula Becker married the good-natured but rather
mediocre artist Otto Modersohn, another member of the
colony. The marriage was not successful, and in February
1906 Paula, who felt that it was strangling her creative
powers, left her husband and went to Paris, from where,
however, her husband persuaded her to return to him at the
end of the year. She died at Worpswede on 21 November
1907, shortly after giving birth to a child.

What made her fate so significant for Rilke was that it
seemed to symbolize in an especially poignant and tragic
fashion that opposition between the claims of art and the
claims of life of which he himself was continually aware. He
found the attempt to be a poet and nothing but a poet so
difficult that he was sometimes tempted to abandon it for
some other profession. The "help" which he begs of her at the
end of the poem may be regarded as help to resist this
temptation.

DUINO ELEGIES

THE FIRST ELEGY

Gaspara Stampa: an Italian poetess (1523–1554) of noble family
who recorded her at first happy and then unrequited love in
some two hundred sonnets.

SONNETS TO ORPHEUS

The *Sonnets to Orpheus* were written as a funeral monument for
Wera Ocukama Knoop at the Château de Muzot, Sierre,
Switzerland, 2–23 February 1922, and were published at the
end of March 1923.

At the beginning of January 1922 Rilke's friend Frau
Gertrud Ouckama Knoop had sent him a journal she had kept
during the long and fatal illness of her daughter Wera, who
died at the age of eighteen or nineteen, and whom Rilke had
seen once or twice when she was a child. This beautiful girl
had been an exquisite dancer, but, just before the beginning of
her fatal glandular disease, had suddenly declared that she
neither could nor would dance any longer, and, during the
short time that remained for her, had devoted herself first to
music and then to drawing, as though (in Rilke's words) "the
dancing which had been denied were more and more gently,
more and more discreetly, still issuing from her." His
thoughts about Wera, whose fullness and love of life had
seemed to reach their highest intensity when life was passing
into death, crystallized, as it were, around the figure of
Orpheus with his lyre, of which he had recently acquired a
small engraving—Orpheus the mediator, at home in the
realms both of the living and of the dead; and the result was
this entirely unexpected series of sonnets, of which the First
Part was written shortly before and the Second Part shortly
after, the completion of the *Duino Elegies*.

THIS IS THE CREATURE

The unicorn has anciént, in the Middle Ages continually
celebrated, significations of virginity: hence it is asserted
that, although non-existent for the profane, it *was,* as soon as
it appeared, within the "silver mirror" which the virgin is
holding before it (see tapestries of the fifteenth century) and
"in her," as in a no less pure, no less mysterious mirror.

[Rilke is alluding to the celebrated tapestries of *La Dame à la Licorne* in the Musée de Cluny.]

POEMS 1906–26

To Music
Written after a private concert at the house of the recipient.

When Will, When Will
"Written on the evening before the Orpheus sonnets."

For Witold Hulewicz
Inscribed in the *Duino Elegies* for his Polish translator: "To that
    faithful and active intermediary, Witold Hulewicz (Olwid),
    with gratitude: Rainer Maria Rilke."

R.M.R.
Epitaph composed by himself before 27 October 1925 and
    inscribed on his tombstone in the churchyard at Raron.

INDEX OF TITLES